AKL:INTERMEDIATE

VA, 12 / 05 / 1991

AMERICAN KERNEL LESSONS

AKL:INTERMEDIATE

ROBERT O'NEILL
ROY KINGSBURY
TONY YEADON
EDWIN T. CORNELIUS, JR.

Longman
American English

American Kernel Lessons: Intermediate

Library of Congress Cataloging in Publication Data

American Kernel Lessons: Intermediate

    1. English language—Textbooks for foreigners.
I. O'Neill, Robert.
PE1128.A477   428'.3'4   78–16607
ISBN 0 582 79706 3

Cover Design: Frederick Charles Ltd.
Cover Illustration: Jeffrey F. Feinen
Illustrations for Episodes: Jeffrey F. Feinen
Illustrations for Situations: Pamela Baldwin Ford
Maps: Audrey Sclater

Longman
95 Church Street
New York, New York 10601

Distributed in the United Kingdom by Longman Group Ltd., Longman House, Burnt Mill, Harlow, Essex CM20 2JE, England, and by associated companies, branches and representatives throughout the world.

LMNOP–RA–959493929190

Contents

To the Student and Teacher

Who this book is for

This book is for intermediate students. The authors believe that intermediate students have special problems:

1. Intermediate students often feel that they are not progressing fast enough in English. They sometimes feel that they are not making as much progress as they did when they were at the beginning level.
2. Intermediate students usually realize that they need practice in some of the fundamentals of English. However, they feel that the kind of practice they need is different now, and definitely not the same type they needed when they were beginners.
3. Intermediate students have studied a lot, but they feel they have not *really* learned everything they have studied. In other words, there are many things they have studied which they still cannot seem to use correctly, easily and as automatically as they would like.

In most ways, intermediate-level study is more interesting and more rewarding than beginning level. Students will find that they will actually learn to use things that they have studied before but never really "learned." They will also learn to use many things that are entirely new to them—things they have never seen before. All in all, learning can be a more enjoyable experience now.

How to use this book

The book has 25 units. It will probably take between two and three hours of classroom work for each unit. Some groups, of course, may spend more time on each unit. The units all have five parts, covering six pages:

Part A (2 pages) The illustrations given on the first page help students understand the "situations" on the second page. These situations contain examples of the new structures introduced in the unit. In classroom study, the first step will be to cover the situations on the right-hand page and to work with the illustrations on the left-hand page. The teacher will read each situation aloud or play the cassette as the students listen and study the illustrations. In studying Part A, the following should be remembered:

1. The situations themselves are more important than isolated words. Students should listen to each situation and try to understand the whole situation—even if they do not understand certain words.
2. Students can learn to write the words correctly later on. First, they should learn to use them correctly and pronounce them correctly.
3. Students are encouraged to take an active part in the intensive question-answer practice in class. They should not be afraid of making mistakes.
4. After students have practiced questions and answers with the teacher, they should be able to use the cues—the words given next to the illustrations—in practicing questions and answers with other students.
5. After question-answer practice in class, students should uncover the situations and read them silently. Following the "silent reading," there will be time for students to ask questions about problems they encountered.

Part B (1 page) This is the *Formation and Manipulation* page. It focuses attention on important facts about the formation (structure) and pronunciation of the material introduced in the unit. The material given in Part B provides opportunities for intensive oral practice in class and for written practice at home.

Part C (1 page) This is a simple detective story, intended primarily for reading enjoyment and comprehension practice. Each unit has one part or ''episode'' of the story. Each episode is also recorded on tape for listening and comprehension practice. In following the story through the 25 units, students will learn new vocabulary, and will have the opportunity to discuss details of each episode with the teacher and other students.

Part D (1 page) This part of the unit is called *Further Practice.* It includes a number of exercises and a short conversation. After listening to the conversation—read by the teacher or listened to on the cassette—students will have an opportunity to ''role-play'' the conversation in class with other students.

Parts E and F (1 page) These parts are a summary of the things studied in the unit. Special exercises are given for additional practice in class and for homework assignments. An important feature of Part E is *Guided Composition.* This section will help guide students in writing compositions, using the vocabulary and structures they have learned in the unit.

1

a. Jane works / where?

b. What time open?

c. her boss?

2

a. work / where?

b. day shift / time?

c. late / early?

d. time now?

e. wife / always / drive?

3

a. Joe wants / what?

b. Frank's question?

c. Joe's answer?

4

a. What / do?

b. always / play?

c. in movies / does what?

d. real life?

5

a. What / do?

b. live / where?

c. How much money?

d. Who / woman?

6

a. life?

b. always / sleep late?

c. husband's question?

d. answer?

1

Jane Nelson works in the executive office of a big company. The office opens at 9 but she is never there on time. Today she is five minutes late. It is five past nine (9:05). Two typists are talking about her.

"Does her boss know she's always late?"

"No, he doesn't. He's usually late too!"

1. Ask where Jane works.
2. Is she always on time?
3. Why doesn't her boss know she is always late?

2

Frank Martin does not work in an office. He works in a factory and he never gets to work late. The day shift starts at 7 o'clock but he often gets there early. He is ten minutes early today. It is ten to seven (6:50). His wife always drives him to work.

1. Make sentences about Frank with these words:
   a. in an office   c. late
   b. factory   d. early
2. Ask when the day shift begins.
3. What does his wife always do?

3

Joe Freeman wants to marry Frank's daughter, Susan.

"What do you do?" Frank wants to know.

"I'm a bookkeeper. I work in a bank."

"Do you really love my daughter?"

"Yes, I do. I love her and she loves me. We want to get married!"

1. What is Frank's first question and what is Joe's answer?
2. Make sentences about Joe:
   a. bookkeeper   b. bank
3. Make sentences about Joe and Susan.
4. Ask what they want to do.

4

Felix Mendoza is a famous movie star. He plays in westerns. He always plays an outlaw in all his movies. He steals cattle, robs banks and has gun fights. He is mean and tough, and people are usually afraid of him. But in real life he is quite different. He is really a kind and gentle person. He likes people and they like him. He lives on a small ranch in Arizona.

1. Ask what Felix Mendoza does.
2. Make sentences about him:
   a. in westerns   d. real life
   b. outlaw   e. likes people
   c. afraid   f. small ranch

5

Bruce and Laura Foster do not live in a house. They live in a large apartment building in a big city. Bruce is a businessman. He makes a pretty good salary. His wife is very young. They are very happily married.

Ask questions using these words:
   a. a house?
   b. Bruce / a movie star?
   c. good salary?
   d. wife / very old?
   e. happy?

6

Laura leads a very busy life. She never sleeps late in the morning. She always has a lot of things to do. She usually fixes breakfast for her husband.

"Do you need the car today?" her husband wants to know.

"Yes, I do," Laura answers.

1. Ask questions:
   a. stay in bed / mornings?
   b. anything to do?
   c. who fix / husband's breakfast?
2. What is her husband's question and what is her answer?

1b FORMATION AND MANIPULATION

(handwritten: Sự tạo thành) *(handwritten: Sự xử dụng)*

---

1 a. Notice the *s* in verbs with *He, She:*

He She	work*s* live*s* make*s*	in a factory. in an apartment house. a good salary.

Make sentences about your father, mother or friend.

b. Notice how the question is formed: *(handwritten)*

Does	he she	work in a factory? live in an apartment? make a good salary?

Ask someone else questions about his or her father, mother, etc.

---

2 a. Notice verbs (no *s*) with *I, You, We* and *They:*

I You We They	work here. live in San Francisco. make $125 a week.

Make sentences about yourself, your friends, other students, etc.

b. Notice how the question is formed:

Do	you I they we	work here? live there? earn a lot?

Ask your friends or other students questions about themselves.

---

3 a. Notice how the first word of a question is always repeated in the answer:

Question	Answer
Do you live here?	Yes, I *do.* No, I *don't.*
Does he know?	Yes, he *does.* No, he *doesn't.*
Is he a teacher?	Yes, he *is.* No, he *isn't.*

Think of questions to ask the person next to you. Tell that person to give you a short answer.

b. Notice how negative sentences are formed:

Jane Joe	doesn't (does not)	work in a factory.
You I We They	don't (do not)	live on a ranch. get to work before 6 o'clock. earn $12,000 a year.

Make true sentences about yourself and other people with *doesn't / don't.*

---

4 a. Notice the position of these adverbs of frequency: *usually, often, always* and *never:*

1	2	3
She We	never often usually always	gets to work late. get there early.

What are some of the things you often do? Also make sentences with *never* and *always.*

b. Notice the position of frequency adverbs with the verb BE (*am, is, are*):

1	2	3	
She We	is are	always often never usually	late. on time. early.

4

The Man Who Escaped

EPISODE 1

Gordon Fletcher used to be an army officer, but he is in the federal penitentiary in Leavenworth, Kansas, now. Every day is exactly the same for him.

5   It is winter now. Fletcher and all the other inmates get up at five-thirty every morning. It is still cold and dark then. They eat breakfast at six o'clock. Work begins at seven. Some of the men work in the prison factory where they
10 make shoes and metal furniture, but Fletcher often works on road building and road repair jobs outside.

  The men eat lunch at twelve. They have forty-five minutes for lunch and then they go
15 back to work again. Dinner is at six. Fletcher usually goes to the prison library after dinner and often reads until 9:30. The lights go out at ten every night.

  The days are long, hard and boring, and the
20 prisoners have a lot of time to think. They usually think about why they are there. Fletcher does. He always thinks about two men.

  One of the men is John Kincaid. He used to
25 be an army officer just like Fletcher. Fletcher knows that Kincaid has a lot of money now. The second man's name is Hooper. Fletcher only knows the man's name. Kincaid knows where and who Hooper is, but Fletcher
30 doesn't.

  Every night Fletcher lies in his bunk and thinks about John Kincaid and Hooper. There is another thing he thinks about too. Escaping. He wants to escape and find Kincaid and
35 Hooper. Fletcher is an innocent man and he wants to prove it!

1d FURTHER PRACTICE

1 / Invention Exercise

MODEL:

He She	often never always	does that.

CUE: football on Saturdays
RESPONSE: **He always plays football on Saturdays.**
or: **He never watches football on TV on Saturdays.**

Cues: đưa, fán cười, gãy đi đón I bữa.

a. parties on weekends
b. disco music
c. coffee without sugar
d. to work by bus
e. sports magazines
f. picnics in the winter
g. movie on Saturday night
h. detective stories
i. eggs for breakfast
j. vacation in August

2 / Conversation

Joe Freeman likes rock music. He has a good record collection. His friend Ken Grimes is visiting him and Joe is playing his latest record by a new rock group called "The Electronics."

KEN: (shaking his head) Phew! Is that supposed to be music?

JOE: What did you say?

KEN: Is that the kind of music "The Electronics" play?

JOE: Yeah. This is their latest hit. How do you like it?

KEN: It's awful! I don't understand how you can listen to that noise.

JOE: I like them very much. They're playing at Jansen Stadium tomorrow night and I have tickets.

KEN: Have you got any extra tickets?

JOE: Yes, as a matter of fact, I've got three or four. Why?

KEN: Well . . . uh . . . Could I buy a couple of tickets from you?

JOE: You want to buy tickets for the concert . . . ? But you don't like "The Electronics"!

KEN: No, *I* don't. But my girlfriend does and she wants me to take her to the concert.

Questions
1. What does Joe say when he doesn't understand Ken's question?
2. Why doesn't Ken like the new rock group?
3. What does Ken want to do when he hears Joe has extra tickets to the concert?
4. Ask and answer why he wants to do this.

Practice
1. Repeat after the teacher or tape recorder Joe's intonation of *What did you say?*
2. Make some sentences of your own with *Could I . . . . ?*
3. Observe the word order

    1   2   3
I like them very much.
Think of some things you like very much.
Use the same word order.

e / Summary *lề hước*

Focal Points in this Unit

1. Sentences like *He works in a factory, She always has a lot to do* and *They live in a large apartment building* are all in the *Simple Present tense.*

   Notice that in these situations the tense does not tell you what the people are doing at the moment. For instance, in situation 3, Joe says, "I work in a bank." That is not what he is doing at the moment.

   One of the main uses of this tense is to talk about what people often, always, never or usually do. That is why we use it when we want to say what Gordon Fletcher does every day.

2. Remember that *always, often, never* and *usually* go after the verb *BE* and auxiliaries, and in front of the main verb.

   She *is* always late to work.
   He *always gets* there on time.

3. Remember how we ask questions (*Does he work in a factory?*) and how we make negative sentences (*They don't live on a ranch*). Look at the Formation and Manipulation page for examples of these constructions.

   hỏi về nghi nghiệp .

4. The question *What do you do?* or *What does he do?* is often used to ask what a person's job is. It is never used to ask about someone's actions at the moment. For this, we use the question *What is he doing?* and *What are you doing?* (See Unit 2.)

   hỏi về thói quen làm cái gì .

f / Exercises for Homework

1. Make these sentences into questions and then into negative sentences like this:

   Harry works in an office.
   Does Harry work in an office?
   No, Harry doesn't work in an office.

   a. Jane works in a factory.
   b. Bruce and Laura live on a ranch.
   c. Laura is old. *Is Laura old ? No, she isn't*
   d. Bruce and Laura have two cars.
   e. Secretaries lead an easy life.
   f. Felix plays the hero in cowboy films.
   g. Joe and Susan want to get married next year.

2. **Guided Composition**
   Read lines 7 to 18 of the Episode again carefully and then, using the same sentence patterns, write about this person:

   Jane / breakfast / 8:15 / at home // work / 9 // often late //
   Jane works / office // lunch / 12:30 // lunch / an hour//
   dinner / 6:30 // usually / television / after dinner // often read / 10:45 // never / to bed before / 11 o'clock //

3. **Transfer Exercise**
   Write true sentences (at least 4) about yourself, friends and family. Use this pattern:
   I / we . . . never / always . . . .

1

a. What time?
b. What / Laura?
c. What / cat?
d. Where / Frank?
e. the men / music on the radio?
f. What / talking about?

2

a. What / Laura / friends?
b. they / lunch?
c. What / one of them / wearing?
d. Where / Frank?
e. Frank / always / there?
f. What / a lot of men and women?
g. waiting for?

3

a. Where / Bruce and Laura?
b. What / Laura?
c. Why / Bruce / the man?
d. What / Frank?
e. What / wife?
f. What / Susan?
g. Frank / a movie?

4

a. Who / Susan / talking?
b. Where / Joe / from?
c. Susan's questions?
d. What / Frank and his wife?
e. Susan / ready for bed?
f. Where / she?

1

It is nine-thirty (9:30). Laura is ironing some clothes *present continuous* and listening to music on the radio. The cat is sleeping on the kitchen stool.

   Frank is at the factory. The men there are not listening to the radio. They are taking their coffee break. They are talking about the World Series baseball game tonight.

1. Ask questions with these words:
   - a. What / Laura
   - b. the cat
   - c. Where / Frank
   - d. talking about
   - e. the men / radio
2. Make sentences with *isn't* and *aren't*. (Frank / the radio, etc.)

2

It is eleven-thirty (11:30). Laura and her friends are not having lunch. They are having coffee. They are talking about their husbands. One of them is wearing a scarf to cover up her rollers. *Kẹp tóc quấn lại*

   Frank is eating in the cafeteria at the factory. He always eats there. A lot of men and women are standing in line. They are waiting to buy their lunch. It is raining outside.

1. Ask and answer these questions about Laura and her friends:
   - a. lunch
   - b. talking about
   - c. baseball
   - d. Laura / scarf
2. Ask these questions about Frank and the other men:
   - a. restaurant
   - b. Frank / always
3. What are the men and women behind Frank doing and what are they waiting for?

3

whisper: nói thì thào

It is 9 o'clock at night. Bruce and Laura are at a concert. Laura is whispering something to Bruce and he is looking at the man next to her. The man is bothering her because he is snoring. *(breathe audibly in sleep)*

   Frank is watching television but his wife and Susan are not. Susan is reading a book and her mother is writing a letter. Frank is watching a baseball game.

1. Ask and answer questions about Bruce and Laura:
   - a. a baseball game
   - b. Why / whispering
   - c. What / looking at
   - d. Why / bothering
2. Ask and answer these questions about Frank and his family:
   - a. Susan and her mother / television
   - b. Frank / a movie on TV
3. Ask and answer what each person in the picture is doing.

4

It is 11 o'clock (11:00). Susan is talking to Joe. He is phoning from San Francisco. "Are you having a good time? What's the weather like? Is it raining?" she wants to know.

   Frank and his wife are getting ready for bed. He can hear Susan downstairs. "Who's she talking to?" he is asking.

1. What is Susan doing and where is Joe phoning from?
2. What are the questions Susan is asking?
3. Ask what Frank and his wife are doing and what Frank is asking.

2b FORMATION AND MANIPULATION

1 Pronunciation

a. Practice contractions of BE (*'m*, *'s*, *'re*) in these typical examples:

    1. Frank *'s* at the factory. He *'s* working.
    2. They *'re* listening to a concert.
    3. What *'s* she doing?
    4. I *'m* never late for work.

b. Practice full forms of BE (*am*, *is*, *are*) in these questions:

    1. *Am* I speaking too fast?
    2. *Is* the bus coming?
    3. *Are* you waiting for the bus?

2

a. Notice the forms of BE after *he, you, I*, etc.:

I	*am* (*'m*)	learning English.
He She	*is* (*'s*)	watching television.
You We They	*are* (*'re*)	listening to the teacher. disturbing those people.

b. Notice the position of *is, are* and *am* in questions:

Am	I	
Is	my radio	disturbing you?
Are	we	

Make at least six sentences from **2a** into questions.

c. Notice how the negative is formed:

I am (I'm)	
She is (She's)	not listening.
They are (They're)	

Note: *is* and *are* may be contracted either with the pronoun (she's, he's, they're, we're) or with the negative form *not* (isn't, aren't). *She's not / She isn't* and *They're not / They aren't* are alternate forms. Either form may be used. With the pronoun *I*, notice that there is no alternate form for *I'm not*.

Use **2a** again to make two negative sentences each with *He, You* and *I* (six sentences in all).

3

Notice the position of words like *to, at* and *for* (prepositions) in these questions with *Who* and *What*:

What		waiting for?
	are you	looking at?
Who		listening to?

Look at the picture situations again. Start at situation 2 and think of questions like these for the people in the situations.

The Man Who Escaped
EPISODE 2

It is six o'clock on a very cold winter evening. All over the Midwest, people are sitting down in front of their television sets to watch the news. Local stations in Kansas and
5 Missouri have one very important piece of news this evening. It is this:

"Federal authorities and local police are looking for a man who escaped from the federal penitentiary in Leavenworth, Kansas
10 early this morning. The man's name is Gordon Fletcher. He is 30 years old, six feet tall, and has black hair and brown eyes. He is wearing a dark blue prison uniform. The police believe Fletcher is still in the local area."

15 At the Ringside Club in Chicago, the TV at the bar is tuned to Channel 6 News. Most of the people there are not very interested in the news, but one man is. His name is John Kincaid. He is about 45 and he is wearing very
20 expensive clothes. He looks worried. There is another man standing next to him at the bar. Kincaid is asking him a question.

"Did they say the man's name was Fletcher?"

25 "Yes, something like that . . . . Gordon Fletcher. Why? Do you know him?"

"No . . . no, I don't know him . . . I . . . I just wanted to know the man's name, that's all."

30 At 9th and Pennsylvania Avenue in Washington, D.C., a young man is standing in the office of his chief at the Federal Bureau of Investigation. The young man's name is Richard Rossi. He is an FBI agent.

"Do you remember Gordon Fletcher,
35 Rossi?"

"Yes, very well. I arrested him four years ago in Philadelphia."

The chief is nodding his head.

"Yes, I know that, Rossi. That's why I'm
40 giving you this case now. I want you to find Fletcher again! We've got to find him fast!"

2d FURTHER PRACTICE
Khác

1 / Invention Exercise

Make questions using the cues.

CUE: I / too fast?

RESPONSE: **Am I driving too fast?**

or: **Am I speaking too fast?**

Cues:

a. I / your seat?

b. you / a good time?

c. Jane / lunch now?

d. Frank / a baseball game?

e. we / too much noise?

f. you / the news?

g. those people / about me?

h. that woman / a bicycle?

i. Laura / her friends?

2 / Conversation

A TALKATIVE LADY

(The ticket office in a railroad station. We can hear the sounds of trains coming and going and announcements over the loudspeakers.)

LADY: Good afternoon. I'd like some information about the trains, please.

CLERK: Yes, ma'am. Which train? Where are you going?

LADY: To Columbus. You see, I have a sister there and . . .

CLERK: So your question is "When's the next train to Columbus?" Is that right?

LADY: Yes, that's right. When's the next train to Columbus, please?

CLERK: At four thirty-seven. That's in about five minutes.

LADY: Thank you very much. Oh! Can I get something to eat on the train?

CLERK: Yes, ma'am. There's a dining car on the train.

LADY: Oh, good! Uh . . . how much does a cup of tea cost? I find that a cup of tea is good for my nerves when I travel.

CLERK: I'm not sure. Fifty cents, I think.

LADY: Fifty cents! Goodness! Things are getting so expensive!

CLERK: Yes, they are. Excuse me, ma'am. Your train's going to leave in two or three minutes now.

LADY: Thank you. Oh! What track is it on?

CLERK: Track 13.

LADY: Track 13! Oh, dear! I never take a train that leaves on track 13! 13's an unlucky number. When's the next train after this one?

Questions

1. Without looking at the text, ask the questions the lady asked, using these words:

   a. next train to Columbus   c. track

   b. something to eat

2. What does the lady like when she travels? Ask why and answer.

3. What is it that she never does? Ask why and answer.

Practice

Make questions of your own using these two patterns:

a. When's the next . . . to . . . ?

   Cues:

   bus / Pershing Square

   plane / New York

   ship / Tahiti

b. How much does (*do*) . . . cost?

   Cues:

   those jeans

   a quart of milk

   that camera

   that sweater

   those shoes

   a ticket to Miami

e / Summary

Focal Points in this Unit

1. Sentences like *Where are you going?*, *Frank is watching television*, etc., are in the Present Continuous tense.

   Notice that in the situations in this unit, the tense is used to say what people are doing at the moment, at the time you are talking about them. When you want to talk about what they sometimes, always or usually do, you use the Simple Present tense. For instance, in situation 2 on page 9 we say:

   Frank is *eating* in the cafeteria at the factory. He always *eats* there.

2. Study the Formation and Manipulation page carefully. Notice how questions and negative sentences are formed. Notice that in the negative, we can use *not* in its full form or in contractions. We can say:

   He's *not* coming.
   or
   He is*n't* coming.

   They're *not* watching TV.
   or
   They are*n't* watching TV.

3. Notice that we usually use the Simple Present tense when we ask what time a train leaves, or a bus arrives. (See Conversation page 12.) We do this because we are thinking of what the timetable says.

f / Exercises for Homework

1. Answer all the questions and complete the exercises on pages 9 and 10.

2. Notice how these cues are used to make two sentences: Laura / always up / 7:30
   Laura always gets up at 7:30. It is 7:30 now and she is getting up.
   Do the same with these cues (two sentences each):
   a. Frank / breakfast / 6:15
   b. Bruce / to work / 8 o.'clock
   c. Laura / usually lunch / 12:30
   d. Frank / usually / the news / on TV / 10 o'clock
   e. I / the radio / 6 o'clock / morning

3. Make sentences of your own with these words:
   listen to, talk to, talk about, wait for, look at.
   Examples:
   I'm waiting for a bus.
   Jane never listens to the 8 o'clock news.

4. **Guided Composition**
   Read the news item from the Episode again carefully (page 11, lines 7-14) and then, using the same sentence patterns, write another news item with these cues:
   State Highway Patrol / local police / young woman / a jail / Los Angeles, California / late last night // Ginger Franklin // 27 / five feet two inches / blonde hair / blue eyes // light green dress // police believe / still / Los Angeles area //

5. **Transfer Exercise**
   Write 5 true sentences about things that are happening or about what other people are doing now while you are doing this exercise.

1

a. late this morning?
b. eat?
c. drink?
d. the dishes?
e. much time?

2

a. friend's question?
b. Where / boss?
c. When / he / Jane?

3

a. How often / Sacramento?
b. Sacramento / yesterday?
c. friend's question? (on time yesterday?)

4

a. Where / Bruce / this morning?
b. Where / Laura?
c. Laura's question?
d. Who / Bruce / meet?
e. train early?

5

a. Joe and Susan / this afternoon?
b. What / now? (punch / cake / good time)
c. What / Susan's father?

6

a. Who/ at the reception?
b. What / all do?
c. Joe's mother?
d. What / Frank?

He *went*
Did he *go?*
He *didn't go*

He *arrived*
Did he *arrive?*
He *didn't arrive*

3a

1

Jane often gets up late and she got up late this morning. She ate some cereal and drank some coffee. She did not wash the dishes. She left the dirty dishes in the sink. She did not have very much time this morning.

1. Is Jane getting up now?
2. Is she eating cereal and drinking coffee now?
3. List three things she did this morning.
4. What did she do with the dishes and why?

2

Jane is having lunch with a friend. "Were you late again this morning?" her friend wants to know. "Yes, I was, and my boss, Mr. Ellis, was already in his office."
  "Oh? Did he see you?"
  "Yes, he did. He saw me when I came in."

1. What is Jane doing?
2. What question (exact words) did her friend ask and what is Jane's answer?
3. Ask if Jane's boss saw her.
4. Ask when.

3

Bruce often goes to Sacramento. He went there yesterday and he is going there today too. He is talking to an old friend. "Does this train usually get in on time?" his friend wants to know. "Yes, it does, but it didn't yesterday. It arrived late!"

1. Ask what Bruce often does.
2. Ask what he is doing now.
3. Ask what he did yesterday.
4. What is his friend's question?
5. What is Bruce's answer?

4

Bruce is back from Sacramento. He went there this morning. Laura is at the station to meet him. "Did you have a successful trip?" she wants to know. "Yes, I did, and I met an old friend on the train this morning."
  "Did the train get to Sacramento on time?"
  "No, it didn't. It was late again!"
  Ask and answer questions about Bruce:
  a. When / Sacramento   d. Where
  b. a successful trip   e. train on time
  c. When / an old friend

5

Joe and Susan got married this afternoon. They are having the wedding reception now. Susan's parents are there and so are Joe's. They are drinking punch, eating cake and having a good time. Only Joe's mother is unhappy. Susan's father is making a speech.

1. What did Joe and Susan do this afternoon?
2. Ask what they are doing now.
3. Ask questions with: a. eat   b. drink.
4. Ask these questions:
   a. good time   b. Joe's mother
5. What is Frank (Susan's father) doing?

6

Joe and Susan had their wedding reception here this afternoon. Joe's parents were here and so were Susan's. Everybody ate cake, drank punch and had a good time. Only Joe's mother did not eat or drink anything. She was unhappy. Frank made a speech.
  Ask and answer questions with these words:
  a. When / a reception   e. a good time
  b. Joe's parents there   f. Joe's mother happy
  c. Susan's too   g. not eat anything
  d. What / drink and eat   h. Frank / speech

3b FORMATION AND MANIPULATION

1 a. Notice what happens to regular verbs in the past:

> The train usually arriv*es* on time.
> It arriv*ed* late yesterday.
> We usually arriv*e* on time.
> We arriv*ed* late yesterday.

b. Notice how the question and the short answer are formed:

> Did it arrive on time yesterday?
> No, it *didn't*. (Yes, it *did*.)
> Did you arrive on time yesterday?
> Yes, I *did*. (No, I *didn't*.)

Now do this yourself. Make three sentences for each of these, like this:
Jane usually washes the dishes. **She washed them yesterday.**
Did she wash them yesterday?
She didn't wash them yesterday.

1. The train usually arrives on time.
2. We often arrive late.
3. The office usually opens at 9:00.
4. Frank usually watches television.

5. You usually listen to the news.
6. Susan and Joe often talk about money.
7. Bruce often works late.
8. He usually phones her.

2 a. Notice what happens to irregular verbs in the past:

> Arthur often *goes* to Sacramento.
> He *went* there yesterday.
> We often *go* to concerts.
> We *went* to one last week.

b. Notice that we form the question and the negative exactly as we do with regular verbs:

> He *went*.
>
> *Did* he *go*?   He did*n't* go.

Now do this yourself, like this: He went to Sacramento.
When (why, how) did he go to Sacramento?

1. Jane got to the office.
2. Joe and Susan got married.
3. They had a party.

4. They drank all the punch.
5. I ate all the cake.
6. Frank made a speech.

3 Notice when we use *was* and when we use *were*. Also notice the question form and the short answers:

I He She It	was	late here in London early	yesterday. last week. last month.
You We They	were		

Question: Was the train late yesterday?
Answer: Yes, it was. (No, it wasn't.)

Make sentences from this table with all the different pronouns.
Then turn to the person next to you and ask questions with ''Were you . . . ?''
Tell that person to give a short answer.

The Man Who Escaped
EPISODE 3

It is 6:30 in the evening now and it is getting colder. The wind is blowing and it is beginning to snow. About 10 miles away from Leavenworth, a man is hiding in a field. His clothes are
5 torn and wet and he is shivering.

A dog is barking somewhere in the distance. Is it a police dog? He does not know. He only knows one thing: he must find food and some warm clothes. But where . . . ?

The plane is taking off now. Rossi is looking out of the window. He can see lights in the windows of all the apartments and houses around Washington. It is dinner time for most
25 people and they are sitting down to eat in their comfortable homes.

The man next to Rossi is saying something.

"The paper says the man was a spy and that
30 he gave away important military secrets. I sure hope the police catch him!"

"Yes, I do too."

10 At Washington National Airport, Rossi's plane for Kansas City is waiting to take off. There is a man sitting beside him. Rossi does not know the man, but he can see he wants to talk. The man is holding a newspaper in his
15 hands.

"I see someone escaped from Leavenworth this morning."

"Oh, is that right?"

"Yes . . . Do you want to read about it? It's
20 all here in the paper."

"No, thanks."

3d FURTHER PRACTICE

1 / Invention Exercise

1. Use the cues to make sentences:

   CUE: to Los Angeles last Thursday
   RESPONSE: **I went to Los Angeles last Thursday.**
   or: **We drove to Los Angeles last Thursday.**

   Cues:
   a. late yesterday morning
   b. toast for breakfast yesterday
   c. television last night
   d. out for a walk last Saturday
   e. a good time at the party last night
   f. the news on the radio yesterday
   g. a good movie last night
   h. tennis last Wednesday afternoon
   i. married in 1974
   j. 3 cups of coffee this morning

2. Now use the same cues as in (1) to make negative sentences:

   CUE: to Los Angeles last Thursday
   RESPONSE: **I didn't go to Los Angeles last Thursday.**
   or: **They didn't drive to Los Angeles last Thursday.**

3. Now ask questions using the same cues as in (1):

   CUE: to Los Angeles last Thursday
   RESPONSE: **Did you go to Los Angeles last Thursday?**
   or: **Did he drive to Los Angeles last Thursday?**

2 / Conversation

Joe and Susan are in Joe's old sports car. They are at a gas station.

JOE: Three gallons of Super, please.
ATTENDANT: Three gallons of Super. Yes, sir.
SUSAN: Joe . . . why don't we get a small economy car?
JOE: What? You mean sell my sports car? Never!
SUSAN: But it's old and expensive to run. We can't afford it, Joe . . .
JOE: It's a very good car, and we never have any trouble with it at all!
SUSAN: Joe! We had trouble with it only last week. Don't you remember?

ATTENDANT: Uh . . . excuse me. That's $1.95.
JOE: Here you are. Oh, and would you check the battery, please?
ATTENDANT: Check the battery? Sure.
SUSAN: And also, as I remember, it broke down just before we got married and was in the repair shop for a whole week!
JOE: But this is a wonderful car! For one thing, it always starts right up as soon as you turn on the ignition.
ATTENDANT: The battery's okay.
JOE: Thank you.
SUSAN: It sure took a long time to start yesterday morning!
JOE: That was only because it was so cold yesterday morning! It has a wonderful engine. Just listen to it when I start it up now! (He turns the key. The engine turns over but does not start.)
SUSAN: I'm listening, Joe . . .

Questions

1. How does Joe ask the attendant to put gas in the car?
2. What does Susan say about the car?
3. What happened to the car just before they got married?
4. What happened yesterday morning? What explanation does Joe give?

3e/f

e / Summary

Focal Points in this Unit

1. *Ate, drank, washed, arrived*, etc., are all verbs in the Simple Past tense.

2. We use the Simple Past tense with past time expressions, like *yesterday, last week, last Friday*, etc.

3. Sometimes we do not actually put these time expressions in the sentence. They are only in our minds. We still use the Simple Past tense.

4. There are two main types of verbs.
   a. Regular verbs: wash*ed*, watch*ed*, play*ed*
   b. Irregular verbs: see/*saw*, get/*got*, go/*went*, etc.

5. We use the same system to form questions and negatives in the past as we do in the Simple Present. In other words, the past form of *do / does*, which is *did*, is used with the main form of the verb. For example:
   He went there.
   He *did* not *go* there. (He *didn't go* there.)
   Did he *go* there?

6. *Was* and *Were*, of course, do not use the auxiliary *did*. Just like *Am / Is / Are*, questions are formed by moving the verb form in front of the subject, and the negative is formed with *not*. For example:
   Was he here yesterday?
   He *was* not (*wasn't*) here yesterday.

   Were you there last week?
   We *were* not (*weren't*) there last week.

7. In speaking, we usually use the contracted form of *not*. For example:
   He did*n't* come. He was*n't* here.

f / Exercises for Homework

1. Answer all the questions and complete the exercises on pages 15 and 16.

2. Make questions with "What / Where / When did you / they, etc. . . . ?" to which the following cues are possible short answers.
   Example:
   CUE: On the train
   You write: **Where did you meet him?**
   or: **Where did you see her?**
   or: **Where did he read that newspaper article?**
   Cues:
   a. Last Saturday   f. Cereal
   b. About 11:30   g. In September 1975
   c. To a concert   h. A new radio
   d. At the station   i. Last summer
   e. In Los Angeles   j. Ice cream, of course

3. **Guided Composition**
   Read situations 1 and 3 (page 15) again carefully, and then write about this person, using the cues:
   Tom Johnson / often / Philadelphia // there today / last Monday too // late this morning // only time / coffee // flight to Philadelphia / late too// left 10 o'clock / usually / 8:45 //

4. **Transfer Exercise**
   Write 5 true sentences about places you went to, things you did or people you met yesterday.

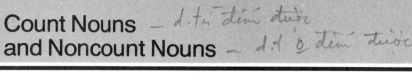

1

a. Bruce / factory?

b. newspaper reporter's questions? (employees? / money? / hours?)

2

1956 $80 A WEEK 48 HOURS $60 A WEEK 40 HOURS

a. When / in a factory?

b. 36 hours?

c. How much / earn?

d. Where / Joan?

e. she / 48 hours?

f. she / $100?

3

1958

a. What / 1958?

b. Why / job?

c. Why / Bruce / better job?

4

1959 $550 A MONTH 40 HOURS A WEEK

a. When / Bruce better job?

b. hours?

c. earn?

d. What / buy?

5

1968 FOSTER SHOE CO.

60 HOURS A WEEK $12,000 A YEAR

a. own factory?

b. How many hours?

c. money?

d. life easier?

e. furniture?

f. small car?

g. wife / car?

6

1971 1976

a. What / 1971?

b. Who / come?

c. Who / children?

d. When / Bruce / Laura?

e. When / they / married?

$150-$300 40 HOURS A WEEK

1

Bruce owns a shoe factory. A newspaper reporter wants to write an article about it.

"How many employees do you have?"
"About 200."
"How much do your employees earn?"
"From $150 to $300 a week."
"How many hours do they work?"
"40 hours a week."

1. Why is the reporter asking these questions?
2. Ask the same questions:
   a. employees   b. earn   c. hours

2

Before Bruce started his own factory, he worked for somebody else. He started in 1956. He worked 48 hours or more a week. He never made more than $80 a week. His first wife was living then. Her name was Joan and she had a job as a salesclerk in a department store. She worked 40 hours a week and made $60. Life was not easy.

1. What did Bruce do before he started his own factory?
2. What did his wife do?
3. Ask these questions about them both:
   a. hours a week   b. earn

3

Joan had to give up her job in 1958 when she had a baby. She did not want to, but she had to. She often said, "You have to find a better job, Bruce. You simply have to!"
   Bruce had to find a better job because they did not have enough money to live on.

1. What did Joan have to do in 1958?
2. Ask why.
3. What did she often say?
4. Why did Bruce have to do this?

4

Bruce came home one day in 1959 and said, "I found a better job today." "Oh? How many hours a week do you have to work? How much do you earn?" Joan asked. "$550 a month for 40 hours a week," he said. That year they had another child, and they bought a bigger house.

1. Ask and answer questions with "When . . . ?"
   a. home and say "I found a better job today"
   b. another baby
   c. a bigger house
2. Ask questions with "How much / How many . . . ?"
   a. hours a week
   b. money a month
   c. children at the end of the year

5

Bruce started his own small factory in 1968. He had to work 60 hours a week at first, but he made $12,000 that year. Life was not easier but it was better. He spent $2,000 on new furniture for the house and bought a bigger car. His wife had a car too.

1. What happened in 1968?
2. How many hours a week did he have to work at first?
3. Ask questions with: a. cars   b. furniture

6

His wife died in 1971. His children were young and his sister had to come and live with them. She had to look after the children. He met Laura in 1976 and married her the same year. Laura is his second wife.

1. What happened in 1971?
2. What did his sister have to do?
3. Ask why.
4. What happened in 1976?
5. Is Laura his first wife?

4b FORMATION AND MANIPULATION

1 Notice the words that go with *How much* and those that go with *How many*:

How *much*	time money gas bread milk	do you have? have you got?		How *many*	cups of coffee glasses of juice cookies pieces of toast	did he have?

Which of these words do you think go with *How much* and which with *How many*? Make questions with "... do you have? / do you want?"

1. chocolate
2. pieces of candy
3. bread
4. sandwiches
5. eggs

6. bacon
7. beef
8. steaks
9. flour
10. pounds of flour

11. glasses of milk
12. children
13. gas
14. baggage
15. suitcases

2 Look at this:

Frank *has to* I *have to*	He get up early every day. *had to* get up early yesterday. I

a. Make sentences like this about someone you know (and about yourself).
    Example: **My sister has to practice her violin every afternoon at this time and**
                I have to listen to it. She had to practice it yesterday and I had to listen to it.
b. How do you ask questions with this form? If you don't remember, look at situation 3. Ask some questions yourself. Use words like *you, your brother, our teacher.*
c. What is the past form of questions with *have to*? Look at situation 5, question 2. Then ask someone else questions like that with:
get up early yesterday, do a lot of homework last week, work very hard when you were in high school, etc.
Notice that the answers are *Yes, I did* or *No, I didn't.*

3 Look at this:

He *found* a better job.	When *did* he *find* a better job?

Ask the same sort of question with these verbs, all of which are from the situations on page 21: *earned* $12,000, *came* home, *bought* a new house, *said* "I found a better job today."

The Man Who Escaped
EPISODE 4

SUMMARY: (NOTE: *From this point on, there is a summary at the beginning of every episode. The summary tells in a few words what happened in the last episode.*) *A young FBI agent, Richard Rossi, arrested Fletcher four years ago. Fletcher escaped this morning from the penitentiary because he wants to find two men, John Kincaid and someone called Hooper. That is all Fletcher knows about the second man. He knew Kincaid when they were officers in the army. Rossi, the FBI agent, left Washington the same day Fletcher escaped. His job is to catch Fletcher again.*

Rossi got on the plane at 7:00. An hour later,
he was asleep on the warm plane. Fletcher was
still in his hiding place in a field 1,000 miles
away. It was getting darker and colder.
5 Fletcher was hungry and tired, and his arms
and legs were so cold that he could hardly feel
them. He knew he had to find food, warm
clothing and a warm place to stay. "I have to
make a move! I can't just stay in this field and
10 freeze to death!" he thought.

Fletcher got up and began to walk through
the field. All of a sudden he saw a faint light in
the distance. "It must be a house!" He could
see the shape of the roof in the darkness.

15 Ten minutes later he came to an old farm. He
stopped and listened "Strange!" he thought,
"I can't hear anything, not even a radio or a
TV, but there must be someone in there!
There's a light on . . ." Just then, he had a
20 terrible thought.
"This is the only house around for miles!
The police know I'm probably around here
somewhere; and if they're anywhere, they're
in that house waiting for me!"
25 Fletcher did not move. The wind was getting
colder. His hands and feet felt like ice. "I have
to take the chance! I have to! This is the only
place I can find warm clothes and food!" he
thought.

4d FURTHER PRACTICE

1 / Invention Exercise

You are talking to Joe Freeman about his job. He works as a bookkeeper in a bank, remember. Ask him questions with "How much / How many . . . ?" using the cues.

CUE: employees / at the bank
RESPONSE: **How many employees are there at the bank?**
CUE: vacation / every year
RESPONSE: **How much vacation do you get every year?**

Cues:
a. free time / every week
b. vice presidents / at the bank
c. work / at the bank every day
d. people / bookkeeping department
e. meetings / every week
f. time / lunch every day

Now use the same cues again to ask questions about *last year, yesterday, last week*, etc.

2 / Conversation

Joe and Susan bought a house last month. They don't have very much money and Susan is adding up all the money they spent on food and other things last week.

SUSAN: We spent $60 last week. $60! That's too much!
JOE: Oh, that reminds me . . . ! We need to get some things for Saturday night.
SUSAN: What things? What do you mean?
JOE: Uh . . . didn't I tell you about the people I invited to dinner?
SUSAN: No, you didn't! What people?
JOE: Well . . . uh . . . you see, there's a tradition at the bank. When an employee gets a promotion, he has to . . . that is, he's supposed to . . .
SUSAN: ". . . give a dinner party"? Is that what you're trying to say?
JOE: Yes. Everybody always does it. So I guess we need to buy some things . . .
SUSAN: You mean, people are coming to dinner *this*

Saturday? Joe . . . ! This is Thursday already. Why didn't you tell me about it before this?
JOE: Well, I don't know . . . I suppose I forgot. I'm sorry . . .
SUSAN: Oh, well, I suppose if we have to give a dinner party, we have to. That's all there is to it. How many people are coming?
JOE: Several . . .
SUSAN: What do you mean? How many did you invite? Only three or four, I hope.
JOE: Well . . . more than that, actually. Now, don't worry about the money . . .
SUSAN: What do you mean, "Don't worry about the money"? Somebody has to! You never seem to worry about it! Now, tell me how many people you invited to dinner!
JOE: Well, naturally . . . I had to invite all of the employees, not just certain ones. I had to!
SUSAN: All of the employees . . . ? How many are there?
JOE: Not many, really . . . 35, not counting the three vice presidents and the manager.
SUSAN: What! 35 people? You must be kidding! It's not just food we need for Saturday night!
JOE: I don't understand. What do you mean?
SUSAN: We need a bigger house!

Correct these statements
STATEMENT: They spent $50 last week.
RESPONSE: **No, they spent $60!**
1. They have to give a party because they bought a new car.
2. They have to give the party next week.
3. Joe often worries about money.
4. Joe invited only some of the employees.
5. Susan thinks they need a bigger kitchen.

Now ask and answer the questions:
1. Ask when they have to give the party.
2. Ask why.
3. Ask what they need for the party.
4. Ask questions with *How much* or *How many*:
   a. employees at the bank
   b. money spent last week
   c. people for dinner on Saturday night

e / Summary

Focal Points in this Unit

1. *How many* is used with count nouns, that is, with words for objects that can be counted (1, 2, 3, 4, . . .). Typical count nouns are *pencil / pencils, man / men, suitcase / suitcases, glass / glasses, bottle / bottles, coin / coins, minute / minutes*, etc.

2. *How much* is used with noncount nouns, that is, with words for objects that cannot be counted. Typical noncount nouns are *money, time, water, flour, bread, sugar, coffee, milk*, etc. These objects can be counted only if they are used in expressions like *glass of . . . , piece of . . . , slice of . . . , bottle of . . . , pound of . . . , jar of . . .* , etc.
Examples: a glass of milk / two glasses of milk, etc.

3. a. *Have to* (*has to*) means "It is necessary to . . ."
   b. The past of *have to* (*has to*) is *had to*.
   c. Questions are formed with *Do / Does . . . have to . . . ?* in the present, and *Did . . . have to . . . ?* in the past.
   d. The future of *have to* is *I will have to . . .* (*I'll have to . . .*) or *I'm going to have to . . . .*

4. *Have to* and *must* sometimes have the same meaning, but there are many differences in the way we use them. You will learn these differences as you gain more practice and experience in English. However, notice these points:
   a. For *must* we use *had to* to express the past and we use *will have to* or *going to have to* to express the future.
   b. We usually use *have to* rather than *must* to talk about necessity. A common situation in which we use *must* is when we give someone very strong advice, such as "You know, you really *must* get a good education" or "You *must* save some money."

f / Exercises for Homework

1. Answer the questions to the situations on page 21 and do the exercises on page 22.

2. In English, we can say "How many children do you have?" or "How many children have you got?" using *have got* instead of *have*. In general *have got* is more informal than *have*. Ask questions with "How much / How many . . . has he / have you got?" and "How much / many . . . does he / do you have?"

   CUE: children / they
   RESPONSE: **How many children do they have?**
   or: **How many children have they got?**
   CUE: money / he / in the bank
   RESPONSE: **How much money does he have (has he got) in the bank?**

   Cues:
   a. friends / they
   b. cars / they / in that garage
   c. boyfriends / she
   d. records / you
   e. rooms / you / in your house
   f. brothers / your friend
   g. meat / we / in the freezer
   h. modern furniture / they / in their house
   i. children / your sister
   j. clothes / she

3. **Guided Composition**
   Read again what happened to Bruce from 1956 to 1968 (situations 2, 3, 4 and 5—page 21), then write about this person:
   Jim Brent / teacher / language school / 1955 // 30 hours a week / $400 a month // wife / bakery // 40 hours / $300 a week // she / give up / 1959 / baby // Jim / better job / money // new house / 1961 / wife / another baby // own school / 1963 // Jim / 55 hours / but / $8,200 // another new house / new car // wife / new car too //

4. **Transfer Exercise**
   Write at least 5 true sentences about things you have to do today or tomorrow, or about things you had to do yesterday or last week.

5a Some, Any, A Few, A Little

1

a. demonstrators?
b. policemen?
c. local people?
d. tourists?
e. reporters?
f. children
   interested?

2

a. What / Susan?
b. What / usually
   use?
c. How much sugar
   always?
d. chocolate?

3

a. When / strike?
b. Where /
   policemen and
   pickets?
c. What day?
d. What / most of
   the men?
e. reporters there?

4

a. What / Bruce /
   order?
b. waiter bring?
c. many people?

5

a. How many men?
b. any women?
c. What time / last
   race?
d. What / Fred?
e. What / want?
f. Fred / any
   money?

1

This is a small demonstration in a park in New York. There are some demonstrators in the park. There are some policemen there too, but only a few. There aren't any local people but there are a few tourists. There are also some reporters there; in fact, there are quite a few. There are also some children in the park but they are not very interested in the demonstration.

1. Ask questions with "Are there any . . .?"
   Answer with *some* or *not any*:
   a. policemen   d. demonstrators
   b. tourists   e. reporters
   c. local people   f. children
2. Now ask questions with "How many . . . are there?"
   Answer with *a few* or *quite a few*.

2

Susan wants to bake a cake, but she doesn't like to use cake mixes. She has some eggs, butter, sugar, milk and flour. She usually uses only a few eggs and just a little butter. She always uses a lot of sugar. She doesn't have any chocolate. She needs some. She wants to bake a chocolate cake.

1. What does Susan want to do?
2. Ask questions with *any*:
   a. eggs   c. sugar
   b. butter   d. milk
3. What does she need? What is it she doesn't have? Why does she need it?
4. Ask "How much / many . . . does she use?"

3

This strike began last week and it is still going on. There are some pickets and some policemen in front of the factory but only a few. It is Saturday and most of the men are watching a football game. The strange thing is that there aren't any reporters or television cameramen there; perhaps they are at the game too.

1. Ask questions with *any*:
   a. pickets   c. policemen
   b. TV cameramen   d. soldiers
2. Are there a few or quite a few people here?
3. Where are all the others?

4

Bruce ordered a steak with some salad and potatoes. The waiter brought him some salad with his steak a few seconds ago but he did not bring him any potatoes. Bruce is asking the waiter to bring him some now. This is Bruce's first time in this restaurant and he wonders why there are only a few people there. Maybe the food is not very good.

1. Ask what Bruce ordered and what the waiter brought him.
2. What is Bruce telling him and why?
3. Ask how many people there are.

5

There are quite a few men at the race track. There are also a few women. It is almost time for the last race (5 o'clock). The man looking at his wallet is Fred Collins. He wants to bet $2 on the last race. The trouble is he doesn't have any money left.

1. Ask questions with "Are there any . . . ?" or "Is there any . . . ?"
   a. men   c. money in Fred's
   b. women   wallet
2. What is Fred doing and why?

5b FORMATION AND MANIPULATION

1 Study this. Notice when we use *is a*, *is some* and *are some*:

There *is a* (There's a)	piece of bread package of jello carton of milk cup detective	over there.

There *is some* (There's some)	bread jello milk food	over there.

There *are some*	pieces of bread packages of jello cartons of milk cups detectives	over there.

Now use one of these three models for these words:

1. oil
2. two bottles of oil
3. glass of orange juice
4. hot coffee
5. warm clothes
6. warm jacket
7. police dog
8. policemen
9. hot water
10. food
11. sandwich
12. sandwiches

2 Study the use of *any* in:

a. Negative sentences

There isn't *any* (There's not *any*)	food coffee money	left.
There aren't *any*	sandwiches potatoes cookies	

b. Questions

Is there *any*	food coffee money	left?
Are there *any*	sandwiches potatoes cookies	

a. Use these tables to make more sentences of your own.

1. I didn't use
2. Do you have
3. They didn't want
4. Did you get

b. Make sentences with these words:

5. Did she buy
6. She didn't buy

3 Study the use of *a little* and *a few*:

There is (There's) We have We've got	only *a little*	work. time. money. gasoline. butter.

There are We have We've got	only *a few*	movie theaters. good hotels in town. cheap restaurants here. serious students. big factories.

Can you make some sentences of your own, with words like: beef in this beef soup, good bookstores here, parks in Washington, D.C., water in the thermos?

The Man Who Escaped
EPISODE 5

SUMMARY: *Fletcher escaped from the penitentiary and hid in a field. It was very cold and he knew he had to find warm clothes and food somewhere. He found a lonely farmhouse. He waited outside the house. He could not understand why there was no noise inside.*

bay hold strick

vua
lua

There was a light in the front window and smoke was coming from the chimney. "Why is it so quiet? Is it a trap? Are the police waiting for me in there?" he asked himself. "If the
5 police are in the house, there must be a police car parked nearby." Slowly he walked through the snow to the back of the house. There was an old barn. He pushed the door open quietly. He saw an old truck there but no police car.
10 He went back to the front of the house and tried the front door. To his surprise it was open! He went in very quietly and looked around. There was a fire burning in the fireplace. The room had very little furniture—a
15 sofa, a table in front of the fireplace and two old-fashioned chairs. It was a small room, but most important of all, it was warm. There were some old photographs on the mantle over the fireplace—one of a young soldier, and several
20 of the same man with a woman in old-fashioned clothes.

Suddenly Fletcher froze. There was some-one else in the room. He knew it. He could feel it! He turned around quickly and saw an old
25 woman coming toward him. She had a covered dish in her hands and there was a delicious smell of meat and vegetables coming from it. She did not look afraid. She did not even look surprised to find a stranger inside her house.

30 "I'm sorry," she said, and then she set the dish on the table. "I didn't hear you knock. I'm deaf, you see." She pointed to her ear, shook her head and said "deaf" a second time.

"People often come to the door and knock, but
35 I don't hear them. I'm glad you came in."
Fletcher looked down at his clothes. They were so dirty that it was impossible to tell that they were prison clothes. Then suddenly he had an idea.

40 "I'm a mechanic from a garage in town. I came out here to fix someone's car, but the road was icy and I wrecked my truck."
He had to say this several times before she finally understood him. When she did, she
45 showed him where to wash up and then she gave him some food. The only thing he needed now was a change of clothes!

5d FURTHER PRACTICE

1 / Special Transformation Exercise

MODEL: I need some eggs.
CUE: We don't have
RESPONSE: **We don't have any eggs.**
CUE: lemonade
RESPONSE: **We don't have any lemonade.**

Cues:

a. sugar	e. I'd like	i. There wasn't
b. There isn't	f. breakfast	j. good movies
c. potatoes	g. We didn't have	k. I saw
d. coffee	h. rain	l. They went to

2 / Conversation

Bruce and his accountant, Don Anderson, went to a small town on the coast near Depoe Bay last week. They went on business and they had to spend the night in a small motel. They had to eat in the motel restaurant too.

DON: Can't we eat somewhere else, Bruce? Very few small places like this serve good food.

BRUCE: I know, but it's late and this place is convenient. Ah! The waiter's coming over for our order now.

WAITER: Good evening. Would you like to order now? I can recommend the roast beef. It's very good.

BRUCE: No, I'm afraid I don't like roast beef. Let me see . . . what else is there on the menu? You go ahead and order first, Don.

DON: All right. Roast beef for me, please. But I don't want any potatoes. I'm trying to lose weight.

BRUCE: I think I'd like fish. Yes, some salmon, please.

WAITER: Uh . . . I'm afraid we don't have any salmon this evening. The roast beef's really very good!

BRUCE: No. If you don't have any salmon, I'd like sole.

WAITER: I'm really sorry, but I'm afraid we . . . uh . . .

BRUCE: You mean you don't have any sole either?

WAITER: No, I'm afraid not.

BRUCE: Well . . . hmm . . . I suppose you have ocean perch, then?

WAITER: Did you say ocean perch?

BRUCE: Yes, that's right, I'll just have perch with some . . .

WAITER: There's very little good perch at this time of the year. Our roast beef's much better!

BRUCE: I'm sure it is, but I don't like roast beef. I'd still like . . .

WAITER: Why don't you just try the roast beef?

BRUCE: Why? Because I don't like roast beef! I never eat roast beef! In fact, I hate roast beef!

WAITER: Well . . . I'm afraid we don't have anything else tonight.

Questions

1. Where does Don want to eat and why can't they do this?
2. Ask and answer these questions:
   a. How many small places / good food?
   b. Why / Don / potatoes?
3. Ask and answer why Bruce can't get any
   a. salmon   b. sole   c. ocean perch
4. What does the waiter say about the roast beef?
5. Why doesn't Bruce want it?

e / Summary

Focal Points in this Unit

1. When we have an idea of the quantity of something but we do not think it is necessary to give the exact amount, we use *some*. We use *some* in-affirmative sentences, with both count nouns and noncount nouns:
   Examples:
   There are *some* policemen in the park.
   There is *some* bread on the table.

2. When we ask questions about something or a number of things, and we have no idea of the quantity, we use *any:*
   Examples:
   Is there *any* food left?
   Are there *any* sandwiches for me?

3. We use *any* (instead of *some*) in negative sentences:
   Examples:
   There isn't *any* food left.
   There aren't *any* policemen in the park.

4. *a few* and *a little:*
   a. *a few* means a small number, and we use it with count nouns—a few policemen / a few people / a few pickets. We sometimes add the word *only* (*only a few*) to emphasize the small number, or *quite* (*quite a few*) to indicate a larger number.
   b. *a little* means "a small quantity," and we use it with noncount nouns—a little sugar / a little gasoline / a little food. We also add the word *only* (*only a little*), or the word *quite*. *Quite a little sugar* means "more than only a little."

f / Exercises for Homework

1. Ask the questions to the situations on page 27, and do the Special Transformation Exercise on page 30.

2. Make statements and ask questions about the following things:
   Example:
   CUE: Good detective novels in that bookstore

RESPONSE: **There are some good detective novels in that bookstore.**
   Are there any good detective novels in that bookstore?

Cues:
a. money in his checking account
b. bread in the breadbox
c. tomatoes in that basket
d. milk in the refrigerator
e. chairs in the room
f. Russian students at the University
g. gas in the tank
h. very good French restaurants in Houston
i. cookies left in the cookie jar
j. time left on the parking meter

3. **Guided Composition**
   Read situations 1 and 3 on page 27 again carefully, and then write about a demonstration last week.
   Use the cues and begin with this sentence:
   There was a small demonstration in a park in New York last week.
   demonstrators / students / policemen // not any local people / but / tourists // reporters / but not many // Saturday / most / football game // also children / park / not interested / demonstration//

4. **Transfer Exercise**
   Write 5 true sentences about yourself using *some* and 5 using *any*. Here are two examples:
   I met some friends downtown yesterday.
   I didn't have any breakfast this morning.

1

a. When / open?
b. What / shoppers?
c. What / salespeople?
d. Where / security guard?
e. What / wear?
f. Who / watch?

2

a. What time?
b. When / close?
c. shoppers?
d. security guard?
e. salespeople?
f. When / last one?

3

a. When / Los Angeles flight?
b. What / want to know?
c. What / answer?

4

a. Why / a hurry?
b. When / main feature?
c. new movie?
d. When / made?
e. When / Jane / movie before?

5

a. Where / Fred?
b. Fred's wife's question?
c. What time?
d. When / he / work?
e. How long ago?

6

a. What time?
b. When / conference?
c. Why / hesitate?
d. What / conference on?

He did something . . . . . years *ago*
hours
How long ago did he . . . .?

6a

1

This is a department store. It is open six days a week, from 9:00 to 5:30. It is closing now. The shoppers are all leaving and the salespeople are counting money. The man in the uniform by the door is a security guard. He is watching everybody.
1. What kind of store is this?
2. When is it open?
3. What are the shoppers doing?
4. Ask why.
5. What else is happening?

2

It is 6 o'clock now. The store closed half an hour ago. All the shoppers left the store half an hour ago. The security guard watched them. Then the salespeople counted their money and went home too. The last one left fifteen minutes ago. That was at 5:45.
1. What did all the shoppers do half an hour ago and why?
2. What did the security guard do?
3. What did the salespeople do?
4. When did the last one leave?

3

Bruce thought the flight to Los Angeles left at 11:30. The fact is that it left at 11:05. It left before he got to the ticket counter. "How long ago did it leave?" he wants to know. "Five minutes ago, at 11:05," the ticket agent replies.
1. What time is it now?
2. What happened before Bruce got to the ticket counter?
3. When did he think it left?
4. Ask two questions about the flight with:
   a. When   b. How long ago

4

Jane and her boyfriend are in a hurry. The main feature started fifteen minutes ago. They do not want to miss too much of it. It is one of Felix Mendoza's old westerns. It was made 15 years ago. Jane does not remember but she saw the film on television a few months ago.
1. Ask and answer why Jane and her boyfriend are in a hurry.
2. Ask how long ago the movie began.
3. How long ago was it made? What year was that?
4. What is it that Jane does not remember?

5

Fred Collins spends most of his time at the race track. We met him in Unit 5. This is his wife. "I wonder where Fred is?" she is saying. Actually she has a pretty good idea. It is 6 o'clock now and she knows he always leaves work at noon on Saturdays. How long ago was that?
1. Is Fred at home?
2. What is his wife saying?
3. Ask these questions about Fred:
   a. most of his time   c. How long ago / work
   b. When / work
4. Where do you think Fred is?

6

Joe does not know whether to go to the conference or not. It is already 3:15 and it started at 3 o'clock. How long ago was that? Joe is hesitating because he does not want to disturb anyone in the conference room. The conference is on income tax regulations.
1. Ask two questions about the meeting:
   a. When   b. How long ago
2. Ask what Joe is doing and why.
3. What is the conference on?
4. Make a sentence of your own with "didn't know whether to . . . or not."

6b FORMATION AND MANIPULATION

1 Notice that the word *ago* comes after phrases like *fifteen minutes, half an hour, 10 years:*

A	B	C	D
They	left	the theater	half an hour	ago.

a. How many words can you think of to replace *They* in box A? (for example: **He**)
b. Now think of words to replace *the theater* in box B.
c. Now look at the situations on page 33 and find other time phrases to replace *half an hour*.
d. Make as many sentences as you can using the words you have for exercises **a, b** and **c**.

2 Notice the question form with *ago:*

A	B	C
How long ago did	the movie	start?

a. Find as many words as you can to replace *the movie* in box B and *start* in box C.
b. Now ask questions with the words you have from exercise **a** and with the words you have from exercise **1c**.
   Answer them like this:
   > *Question:* **How long ago did they go home?**
   > *Answer:* **Ten minutes ago.**

3 Verbs like *start, arrive* and *wash* are regular verbs. They end in *-ed* in the past: *started, arrived* and *washed*.
   Verbs like *leave, see* and *read* are irregular and have different types of past forms: *left, saw* and *read*.

4 You must learn the past forms of regular and irregular verbs by heart. There is a list of verbs at the back of this book. Learn five verbs each day. Start today and learn these verb forms:

Regular:		start–started	look–looked
Irregular:	do–did	get–got	find–found

The Man Who Escaped
EPISODE 6

SUMMARY: *After Fletcher escaped, he hid in a field all day. Then, when it got dark, he found an old farmhouse. There was an old deaf lady in the house. She gave him food. Rossi, the young detective who arrested Fletcher four years ago, flew from Washington to Kansas City. The FBI's orders were, "Find Fletcher immediately!"*

It was a cold, miserable night. In a police station only a few miles from the house where Fletcher met the old woman, two policemen could hear the wind outside. One of them was a
5   young man. The other, a sergeant, was older.
"I wonder how Mrs. Bentley is," the sergeant said.
"Mrs. Bentley? Oh, you mean the old lady who lives on the farm near the Leavenworth
10 road?"
"Yeah. She's deaf, you know. She doesn't have a radio or a TV. Her husband died three or four years ago and she's all alone."
"Oh?" the young policeman said. He won-
15 dered why the sergeant wanted to tell him all this. Then he found out.
"Why don't you go out to her place to see if she's all right?"
"Who? Me? On a night like this?"
20 "It's not far. Besides, you don't have anything else to do. I was thinking about that prisoner—Fletcher. She doesn't know about his escape."

When Rossi got off the plane in Kansas City,
25 there was a detective waiting for him at the airport. He shook Rossi's hand.
"My name's Arnold Wilcox, Kansas City Police Department. We got a wire saying you were coming. There's a car waiting."
30 Rossi wasted very little time on introductions.
"Fletcher escaped this morning. I want to catch him within 24 hours."
Wilcox looked at Rossi for a few seconds.

35 "A lot of us wonder why the FBI is so interested in this guy Fletcher. He isn't the first prisoner to escape. Another man escaped only about six months ago, but the FBI didn't take immediate action then."

40 Rossi was already halfway to the car before he said anything.
"Fletcher isn't just an ordinary prisoner. He's very special. Let's get going!"

The young policeman was angry. He was on
45 the road now. It was icy. Suddenly he lost control and his car went off the road. It was stuck in the snow. "That stupid sergeant!" he thought. "Now I have to radio for somebody to pull me out of the snow!"

6d FURTHER PRACTICE

1 / Invention Exercise

This exercise practices the past tense with *ago*, but we have also added the words *first* and *last*. Notice where we put these words in the model. *First* here means "the first time," *last* means "the last time."

Make sentences using the cues:

MODEL: I $\begin{bmatrix} \text{first} \\ \text{last} \end{bmatrix}$ went to Miami 10 years ago.

CUE: She first / Washington Monument / 3 years

RESPONSE: **She first saw the Washington Monument 3 years ago.**

or: **She first visited the Washington Monument 3 years ago.**

Cues:
a. She last / Miami / 3 weeks
b. They first / the movie / 25 years
c. I last / him / five minutes
d. We last / ice cream and cake / at a party / two weeks
e. Joe and Susan last / a dinner party / about 6 weeks
f. He first / ship / 10 years
g. I first / a novel by James Michener / 6 years
h. She first / my brother / 3 years
i. Bruce last / a new car / 2 months
j. That man first / Paris / 25 years

2 / Conversation

Bruce Foster went out to lunch at 12 o'clock. It's now 2:30 and he's just walking into his office. His secretary is typing. Before Bruce went to lunch, he told his secretary, Miss Bradley, to call him at the restaurant if a man called Mr. Powell came to see him. Bruce came back from lunch only a second ago.

MISS BRADLEY: (nervously) Hello, Mr. Foster. Did you have a good lunch?

BRUCE: Yes, thank you, Miss Bradley. It was very nice. Did anyone call while I was out?

MISS BRADLEY: No. Nobody called, but . . . uh . . . Mr. Powell came by the office.

BRUCE: But he's the man I told you about!

MISS BRADLEY: Yes, I know, but . . .

BRUCE: Well, why didn't you call me? Mr. Powell has some very important business to discuss with me. I wanted to talk to him as soon as possible. I told you all that before I left. Didn't you understand me?

MISS BRADLEY: Yes, of course I understood, but . . .

BRUCE: I even gave you a card with the name and phone number of the restaurant! I put it on your desk.

MISS BRADLEY: But that's just it! You didn't give me the card. You didn't put it on my desk!

BRUCE: What do you mean? Of course I did. I took the card out of my wallet just before I went to lunch! Look! It isn't in my wallet now! (suddenly) Oh!

MISS BRADLEY: Mr. Foster, what's that card on the floor? It fell out of your wallet a moment ago.

BRUCE: That card? Uh . . . it's the card I thought I gave you.

MISS BRADLEY: You see! You forgot! That's why I didn't call. I didn't know where you were.

BRUCE: I'm very sorry, Miss Bradley. It wasn't your fault. I apologize.

MISS BRADLEY: That's all right. Don't worry about it.

Questions
1. Ask (and answer) when Mr. Powell came to the office.
2. Why is Bruce so angry when Miss Bradley tells him this?
3. What does Bruce think he did before he left? Ask and answer if he did. (her / the card / on her desk)
4. Why didn't Miss Bradley call Bruce?
5. What are Bruce's exact words when he apologizes?
6. What is one thing we can say in English when someone apologizes to us?

Practice
Which form of these words do we use in questions in the past? Which form do we use in statements about the past? Make sentences with each one.

a. have / had
b. tell / told
c. call / called
d. understand / understood
e. give / gave
f. know / knew
g. forget / forgot
h. go / went
i. come / came
j. fall / fell

e / Summary

Focal Points in this Unit

1. The word *ago* goes after phrases like *two minutes, three years, a long time, half an hour,* and means a certain time (two minutes, three, etc.) back from now. Remember the examples you have had in this unit:

    It is 6 o'clock now. The store closed at 5:30. That was *half an hour ago.*

2. Use the Simple Past tense with the word *ago:*
    It *left* 5 minutes *ago.*
    The film *was made* 10 years *ago.*
    Bruce *came* back from lunch only a second *ago.*

3. To ask a question with *ago*, we often use *How long ago . . .?*
    How long ago did it leave?
    How long ago was that?

4. Remember how we use the two words *first* and *last* with the Simple Past and *ago.* Look at the Invention Exercise on page 36 again. Here is one example to remind you:
    I *last* saw him 5 minutes ago.

f / Exercises for Homework

1. Do all the exercises and questions on pages 33 and 34.

2. Ask and answer questions using *ago.*

    Example: It is 8 o'clock and I am watching television. I turned it on at 7.
    Q: **How long ago did you turn the television on?**
    A: **I turned it on an hour ago.**
    a. It's March now, and Mary is living in France. She went to France in January.
    b. It's 4:30 now, and Bruce is sitting in his office. He came back from lunch at 2:30.
    c. Tony is standing outside a store. (It's 6:30.) But the store closed at 5:30.
    d. It's 3 o'clock, and Laura is sitting in the airport terminal looking sad. Her plane left for Denver at 1 o'clock.
    e. Tony is staying at the Hilton Hotel. (It's January, 1978.) He last stayed there in July, 1974.

3. **Guided Composition**
    Read the conversation again on page 36. Mr. Powell came by the office while Bruce was at lunch. Write the short conversation between Mr. Powell and Bruce's secretary, using the following cues:
    MR. POWELL: afternoon // Mr. Foster? //
    MISS BRADLEY: afternoon // No / lunch / half an hour//
    MR. POWELL: Where? // important information // must / soon as possible //
    MISS BRADLEY: don't know where // told me / no address or phone number // Mr. Foster / not / card // sorry //
    MR. POWELL: all right / not / fault // tell / call later // Good-bye.
    MISS BRADLEY: really / sorry // tell Mr. Foster // Good-bye.

4. **Transfer Exercise**
    Write 5 or more true sentences about yourself, friends or relatives using the word *ago.*
    Examples:
    I graduated from high school 5 years ago.
    My parents and I spent 2 months in Florida 3 years ago.

1
a. How / short player?
b. How / tall player?
c. What / yesterday?
d. won?
e. lost?

2
a. Where / yesterday?
b. beginning?
c. end of the movie?
d. Why / in the middle?
e. Where / Bruce and Laura?
f. Why / walk out?

3
a. How / piano?
b. How / tennis?
c. good swimmer?
d. How / French and Spanish?

4
a. Fred / bus driver?
b. Why / 3 accidents?
c. worst accident?
d. What / after that?

5
a. How / Bruce / when / younger?
b. How many hours?
c. How / now?
d. How many hours / now?

6
a. What / Carter and Tyler do?
b. How / houses?
c. Why / man / shout?

She's a *good* singer. She sings *well.*
He works *as hard as* his father did.
He drove *so dangerously that* he lost his job.

7a

1

These two often play tennis. The short player is good. He is playing well. The tall one is bad. He is playing badly. One always wins and the other always loses. They also played yesterday. Who do you think won? Who lost?

1. What do these two often do?
2. Ask a question about *now*.
3. What kind of player is the short one?
4. How is he playing?
5. Ask the same questions about the other.
6. What happened yesterday?

2

Jane and her boyfriend went to a movie yesterday. They missed the beginning and they did not see the end. It was so bad that they walked out in the middle.

Laura and Bruce went to a concert. The musicians played so badly that Laura and Bruce walked out.

1. Ask these questions about Jane and her boyfriend:
   a. What / yesterday   c. the end
   b. the beginning   d. Why / in the middle
2. Ask what Laura and Bruce did.
3. How did the musicians play?

3

Carol Stuart speaks Spanish and French perfectly. She plays the piano very well and she sings beautifully. She's a good swimmer and she plays tennis very well. Carol is a senior in high school this year. She is an excellent student and she is active in student affairs. That is why she is president of the senior class.

1. Ask how well she does these things:
   a. tennis   c. piano
   b. French   d. Spanish
2. Make sentences with *good* or *well* about Carol with these words:
   a. swimmer   c. sings
   b. student   d. piano player

4

Fred Collins used to be a bus driver but he isn't anymore. He drove so badly and dangerously that he had three accidents in one month. The worst was when he ran into a police car. He lost his job after that.

1. Is Fred still a bus driver?
2. What can you say about Fred:
   a. as a driver?   b. the way he drove?
3. Ask how many accidents he had. (answer)
4. What was the worst and what happened after that?

5

When Bruce was younger he worked very hard. He worked at least sixty hours a week. He still works hard but not quite as hard as he used to. He works about thirty-five hours a week now.

Ask these questions and answer them:
   a. How many hours / younger?
   b. How many now?
   c. hard then? hard now?
   d. hard as he used to?

6

Bob Carter and Jim Tyler both build houses but Carter builds them much better. He is a much better builder. Tyler builds houses quickly but poorly. Once he built a house in a month. It fell down a month later. The man shouting at Tyler is the man who bought the house.

1. What can you say about Carter's houses and the way he builds them?
2. How does Tyler build his houses?
3. What happened once?
4. Who is the other man in the picture shouting at Tyler?

7b FORMATION AND MANIPULATION

1 Study this. Notice how we use the words *good, professional, fluent*, etc., (adjectives) and the words *well, professionally, fluently*, etc. (adverbs). Also notice their position in the sentence:

He	is a	good professional fluent reckless	pianist. tennis player. Spanish speaker. driver.
She			

He	plays the piano plays tennis speaks Spanish drives	(very) well. professionally. fluently. recklessly.
She		

   a. Make pairs of sentences from the tables above.
      Example: **She's a good pianist. She plays the piano well.**
   b. Make pairs of sentences in the same way with these cues:
      Example: reader (*slow*)　**He's a slow reader. He reads slowly.**
      1. singer (*good*)　2. visitor (*frequent*)　3. driver (*careful*)　4. typist (*rapid*)

2 Notice how we form adverbs from adjectives. There are three main types:
   a. Adverbs made from an adjective + *ly:*
      quick – quickly
      careful – carefully
      dangerous – dangerously
      angry – angrily
      noisy – noisily
      easy — easily
      (NOTE: When the adjective ends in
      -y, change -y to -i before adding -ly.)
   b. Adverbs which have the same form as the adjective:
      hard – hard　　　　　　　　fast – fast
   c. Adverbs which are completely different from the adjective:
            good – well
   Ask another student about himself (or herself), his (or her) friends or relatives using some of the adverbs above
      Example: **Does your father work very hard?**
              Do you drive very carefully?

3

A	B	C	D
He	drove so dangerously	that	he lost his job.

   a. Think of words to replace *drove* and *dangerously* in box B.
   b. Now, with another student, ask and answer questions like this:
      Question: **How dangerously did he drive?**
      Answer: **So dangerously that he lost his job.**

4

A	B	C
He doesn't work	as hard as	he used to.

   a. Think of words to replace *hard* in box B.
   b. Now write four sentences using this structure.

The Man Who Escaped
EPISODE 7

SUMMARY: *Fletcher found an old farmhouse and a woman there gave him something to eat. Rossi arrived at the Kansas City airport. A police detective met him there and asked him why the FBI was so interested in Fletcher. The sergeant at the police station a few miles away from the old woman's farm sent a young policeman to tell her about Fletcher.*

"You poor thing," Mrs. Bentley said to Fletcher after dinner. "You ruined your clothes in the accident! My husband was just about your size, and all of his clothes are up in
5 the bedroom. He died three years ago and they're no good to anybody now. Why don't you see if any of them fit you?" She pointed to the stairway leading to the bedroom.

Fletcher thanked her and went upstairs. He
10 found an old jacket and a pair of pants hanging in the closet. When he came back downstairs, the old woman was sitting in front of the fireplace. She smiled when she looked up at him.

"You know, you look just like my husband
15 in those clothes ... when he was much younger, of course."

Fletcher was thinking about the truck in the barn. He wanted to take the truck and leave quickly. Trying to be polite, he said, "I can't
20 thank you enough. You've been very kind."

The old woman did not understand what he was saying. She shook her head. "Don't worry. There's a truck in the barn. You can use it and bring it back tomorrow."

25 "What do you know about Fletcher?" Rossi asked Wilcox as they drove away from the airport. "Very little," Wilcox said. "They arrested him on a spy charge a few years ago. But that's about all I know."

30 "That's right. But you know, Fletcher always said he was innocent."

"That's what they all say. But what's so special about him?"

"Fletcher was in Army Intelligence. He
35 knew important military secrets. We never understood why he sold them. There wasn't any real motive. And nobody knows who he sold them to. Anyway, he still knows too much, and we have to catch him before he contacts any of
40 his old friends!"

As the truck approached, the young policeman stood in front of his police car and waved his arms to signal for help. Instead of slowing down, however, the truck raced past the police
45 car, throwing wet snow in the policeman's face.

7d FURTHER PRACTICE

1 / Invention Exercise

1. Make your own sentences with the pattern:
   So good (bad, etc.) that . . .
   MODEL: The movie was so bad that they walked
   out in the middle.
   CUE: movie / interesting / twice
   RESPONSE: **The movie was so interesting that I saw it
   twice.**
   Cues:
   a. weather / cold / two sweaters
   b. baseball game / bad / in the middle
   c. music / loud / a headache
   d. service in the restaurant / slow / out
   e. lecture / uninteresting / out
   f. book / good / 3 times

2. Now make sentences with the pattern: *so well
   (badly, etc.) that . . .*
   MODEL: The short man played so badly that he
   lost the match.
   CUE: Fred / dangerously / his job
   RESPONSE: **Fred drove so dangerously that he lost
   his job.**
   Cues:
   a. orchestra / badly / out
   b. she / piano / well / a prize
   c. man / carelessly / 3 accidents in a week
   d. athlete / slowly / the race
   e. Tyler / house / poorly / down
   f. boss / hard / nervous breakdown

2 / Conversation

Susan used the car today. She drove Joe to the bank
this morning and then went to her mother's house. She
is driving Joe back from work now.
JOE: Why are you driving so slowly?
SUSAN: I'm going as fast as I can. The speed limit is
only 35, you know!
JOE: Forget about the speed limit. Nobody drives that
slowly!
SUSAN: Well, I want to drive carefully. There's a lot of
traffic.

JOE: But there was just as much traffic this morning.
You drove a lot faster then!
SUSAN: That's just it. I drove too fast.
JOE: What? You mean something happened after you
dropped me off?
SUSAN: (nervously) I was in the middle of town. I was
in a hurry, and . . .
JOE: Yeah, go on! What happened?
SUSAN: A little girl ran out in front of me.
JOE: You mean . . . you mean . . .
SUSAN: Wait! Listen! The girl was a good distance
away so I didn't have to slow down.
JOE: (relieved) Well, what's so terrible about that?
SUSAN: Just a second. There's more. The little girl fell
down.
JOE: You mean you hit her?
SUSAN: No, but I almost did. I put on the brakes as
hard as I could. I stopped just in time.
JOE: Well, at least you didn't have an accident!
SUSAN: No, but that isn't the only reason I'm driving
so carefully.
JOE: You mean something else happened?
SUSAN: No, but there's a police car behind us. It's
following us, so we can't forget about the speed
limit, can we?

Correct the statements
Example:
There was not as much traffic this morning.
No, there was just as much traffic this morning.

1. Susan is driving very fast now.
2. She drove very slowly this morning.
3. A dog ran out in front of Susan.
4. The little girl was not very far away.
5. Nothing happened when the little girl ran across the
   street.
6. When the child fell down, Susan did not do
   anything.
7. Susan is driving slowly and carefully only because
   she wants to.

e / Summary

Focal Points in this Unit

1. Adjectives (*good, bad, poor, careful, noisy*) are used with nouns and come before the noun: He's *a good worker* / She's *a careful driver*.
   Adverbs (*well, badly, poorly, carefully, noisily*) are used after the verb and answer the question *How?*:
   How does he work? He *works carefully.*

2. Most adverbs are formed by adding *-ly* to the adjective. Notice how certain things change in the spelling:
   a. quick–quickly   (adjective—*ly*)
   b. careful–carefully   (-l—*lly*)
   c. terrible–terribly   (-ble—*bly*)
   d. angry–angrily   (-y—*ily*)

3. Some adverbs have exactly the same form as the adjective:
   hard; fast; early; late.

4. Remember particularly the irregular *good—well.*

5. Use the pattern . . . *so (badly / carelessly, etc.) that* . . . when you want to show the result of an action:
   He drove carelessly. + He lost his job.
   He drove *so carelessly that* he lost his job.

6. Use the pattern *as . . . as* to compare how two people do (or did) the same thing:
   He doesn't work quite *as hard as* his father did.

f / Exercises for Homework

1. Do all the exercises and questions on pages 39 and 40.

2. **Transformation Exercise**
   Example:
   He works hard. His father worked hard too.
   You write:
   He works as hard as his father did.
   a. The new girl types well. The old secretary typed well too.
   b. You speak French fluently. Your teacher spoke fluently too.
   c. He works fast. His father worked fast too.
   d. That boy writes carefully. His brother wrote carefully too.
   e. He talks loudly. The other teacher talked loudly too.

3. **Guided Composition**
   Read situation 4 on page 39 again carefully, and then write about this person:
   Mary / secretary / American company / anymore // type badly / carelessly / at least 10 mistakes / every letter // worst / 30 mistakes / letter for the boss // lost / job //

4. **Transfer Exercise**
   Write 5 true sentences about yourself, relatives or friends using the patterns *so . . . that* and *as . . . as:*
   Examples:
   My father speaks Italian so well that people sometimes think he is Italian.
   My friend works as hard as I do.

1

a. Which man / harder?

b. man with shovel / more money / tractor driver?

2

a. How / both drivers?

b. How / driver number 3 / drive?

c. Who / win?

3

a. Who / best job?

b. Who / hardest?

c. Who / most money?

4

a. How / ski?

b. Who / worse?

c. What / Joe?

d. both beginners?

5

a. What / both men?

b. night?

c. Why / more clearly?

6

a. How / when younger?

b. What / one day?

c. What / woman?

d. How / Joe / now?

Do something {better / worse / faster / more dangerously / more clearly} than . . .

more / the most
less / the least

well / better / the best
badly / worse / the worst

8a

1

One of these men is a tractor driver. The man with the shovel is his helper. They both have to work hard, but one of them has to work a little harder than the other. Which of them do you think it is? The man with the shovel, by the way, earns less money than the tractor driver.

1. Correct the statements:
   a. Only one of the men has to work hard.
   b. The tractor driver earns less than the other man does.
2. Ask and answer the questions:
   a. tractor driver / hard?
   b. as hard as the other man?

2

Both of these drivers are good. Both have fast cars but one of them is driving a little better and faster than the other is. We cannot be sure which of them is going to win the race, but it looks as if Number 3 is going to win.

1. Ask and answer the questions:
   a. both / good   b. both / well
2. What can you say about one of them?
3. Correct the statements:
   a. The driver of three is not driving as well or as fast as seven is.
   b. We can be sure that three is going to win the race.

3

The man with the watch never has to work as hard as the other two do. He has the best job of the three. He earns the most money and does the least work. The man with the shovel has the worst job. He works the hardest but earns the least.

1. Correct the statements:
   a. The man with the watch has to work harder than the other two do.
   b. He earns the least money and does the most work.
2. Who do you think has the worst job? Why?

4

Neither Joe nor Susan can ski very well. They are both skiing very badly at the moment, but she is skiing even worse than he is. At least he is managing to keep his balance. It is hard for both of them. They are both beginners.

1. Correct the statements:
   a. Both Joe and Susan can ski well.
   b. She is skiing a little better than he is.
2. Why can we say Joe is skiing better?
3. Why is it hard for both of them?

5

Both of these men are looking at the moon but neither of them can see it very clearly. It is a rather cloudy night. One of the men can see the moon just a little more clearly than the other can because he has a much bigger telescope.

1. Ask and answer:
   a. What / looking at?   c. very clearly
   b. clear night   d. Which man / more clearly?
2. Ask why one can see it more clearly than the other (and answer).

6

Joe drives a lot more carefully than he did when he was younger. He almost ran over an elderly woman one day. He just missed her. She managed to get out of the way just in time. He drives much more carefully now than he used to.

Correct the statements:
   a. Joe ran over an elderly woman one day.
   b. She did not get out of the way.
   c. Joe still drives very dangerously.

8b FORMATION AND MANIPULATION

1 Pronunciation

REMEMBER: *than* is pronounced /ðən/

Example: Planes now fly faster than (/ðən/) they used to.

2 He drives dangerously, but . . .

A	B	C	D	E
She drives	more	dangerously	than	he does.

a. Put the words *careful, reckless, slow* in their correct forms into box C.

b. Make sentences beginning "He drives dangerously, but . . ." (Remember you can also put other words into box E in place of *he*.)

3 He drives well / fast / badly, but . . .
(Make sentences.)

She drives You drive They drive	better faster worse	*than* [ðən]	he does.

4

That man has	the best the worst	job.
He does	the least the most	work.

Make sentences with *job, house, car, money, time, fun.*

5 Make sentences using *clearly, loudly, efficiently, cautiously.*
(These words are like *dangerously, carefully,* etc. See **2** above.)

The Man Who Escaped
EPISODE 8

SUMMARY: *After Fletcher escaped from prison, he stopped at an old farmhouse. The old woman there gave him food and clothes and lent him her truck. A policeman from the nearest town drove out to the farm to tell the old lady to look out for Fletcher, but his car got stuck in the snow. Fletcher saw the policeman on the road, but he didn't stop the truck to help him.*

The phone rang at Kansas City Police Headquarters, and Wilcox answered it.

"What? Fletcher . . . ? Where?"

Rossi stood up as soon as he heard Fletch-
5 er's name. Wilcox wrote down the words "1968 Chevrolet—blue truck." Then he put the phone down and turned to Rossi.

"Well, we know where your man Fletcher is now. A policeman almost caught him about an
10 hour ago."

"What do you mean, 'almost' caught him? Where is he? What happened?"

Wilcox glanced at his notes and then leaned back in his chair.
15 "Fletcher stopped at an old woman's farm a few miles from here tonight. A policeman went to the house, but it was too late. The woman let Fletcher take her truck. We've got the license number, of course."
20 "We've got to talk to that woman," Rossi said. "But first, you'd better set up roadblocks everywhere! We can't let him get away now!"

Fletcher was driving the truck through Kansas City. He was trying to decide what to do
25 next. He had to get to Chicago. John Kincaid was in Chicago. Maybe he would find Hooper there too. Suddenly he heard a police siren. It seemed to be coming closer, and then it stopped. At the next stop light, he discovered
30 why. He saw two men get out of a police car in front of Police Headquarters. His heart began to beat wildly. There were police cars everywhere. He wanted to get away from there as fast as he could.
35 As Fletcher drove through the intersection, he saw two men on the steps of Police Headquarters. They were not in uniform. One of them, he thought, looked familiar. He was sure he knew him from somewhere. But where . . . ?

8d FURTHER PRACTICE

1 / For Comprehension

Read this short report, and then answer the questions.

An American university is now doing research on the difference between men and women drivers. It seems that women often drive more carefully than men. The research suggests that men drive faster and more recklessly, but that they also react a little bit faster in emergencies. This is perhaps because it seems they concentrate more when they are driving.

Correct these statements (Notice the use of *less* here.):

a. It seems that men drive more slowly than women do.
b. Men drive less recklessly than women do.
c. Men react more slowly than women do in emergencies.
d. Men concentrate less when driving than women do.

Now give complete answers to these questions:

e. What is the university mentioned doing research on?
f. What does the research suggest is the difference in the way men and women drive?
g. What does it suggest is the difference in emergencies?
h. Why is this?

2 / Conversation

Joe and Susan spent a few days in Seattle last month. They left their car at home and stayed in a good hotel in downtown Seattle. They spent a lot of money. This is what happened the day they were leaving for home.

SUSAN: Why do we have to walk to the bus station? And where is it?
JOE: It's just down this street . . . I think.
SUSAN: Look! There's a policeman! Ask him how to get there.
JOE: All right. Excuse me. Can you tell me how to get to the bus station?
POLICEMAN: Yes. Walk down this street and turn left at the second traffic light. Then walk until you come to the river and . . .
JOE: The river?
POLICEMAN: Yes. When you come to the river, there's a bridge. Just walk across it. It's a narrow bridge, so watch the traffic. Follow the signs that say ''To Westside Bus Terminal.'' You can't miss it.
JOE: And is it very far? I mean, how long does it take to walk there?
POLICEMAN: About fifteen minutes, if you walk fast.
JOE: I see. Thank you very much.
POLICEMAN: Not at all.
SUSAN: Fifteen minutes! And with these heavy suitcases too! I think we ought to take a taxi.
JOE: Not at this hour. Look at the traffic. It's moving very slowly. We can get there just as quickly on foot.
SUSAN: Well, I can't possibly carry this suitcase any farther.
JOE: All right. Let me take it, then.
SUSAN: Don't be silly. You can't carry your suitcase and mine as well!
JOE: Yes, I can. The suitcases aren't that heavy . . . hmm!
SUSAN: You see! They're heavier than you thought!
JOE: Perhaps it's not such a bad idea after all.
SUSAN: What isn't such a bad idea?
JOE: Taxi! Taxi!

Questions
1. What is the first thing Joe asks the policeman?
2. What exactly are the policeman's instructions?
3. How long does he say it takes?
4. What does Susan think they ought to do and why?
5. Why doesn't Joe want to do this?
6. What does Joe find out when he lifts the two suitcases?
7. What does he say then and what does he do?

Practice
Practice the pattern *Can you tell me how to get to . . . ?* with someone else. Think of places you both know. Ask the other person questions with the pattern. Then the other person must tell you how to get there, using such phrases as *Walk down / up . . . , Walk this / that way until you come to . . .* and *Go / Turn left (right) at the first / second intersection . . .*

8e/f

e / Summary

Focal Points in this Unit

1. Remember that *than* is pronounced [ðən].

2. Remember the way we form and use adverbs when comparing things:
   a. He drives *more carefully than* you do.
   b. She works *faster than* he does.
   c. He plays tennis *worse / better than* I do.

3. Remember the Superlative forms (for adjectives) we have used in this unit:
   a. He gets *the most* money and works *the least*.
   b. He has *the best / the worst* house.

4. We can add the words *a little, a little bit, much, rather* or *far* to a Comparative:
   a. They react *a little bit faster* in emergencies.
   b. He drives *much more carefully* now than he used to.

f / Exercises for Homework

1. Do all the exercises on pages 45 and 48.

2. Fill in the correct form (adjective or adverb) of the word in parentheses in these sentences:
   Example:
   Maria sings . . . than Jane does. (good)
   (You write **better,** because this is the form of the word [adverb] needed here.)
   a. He plays the violin much . . . than John does. (good)
   b. Margaret types . . . than Mary does. (fast)
   c. He's a . . . driver. He had another accident last week. (careless)
   d. This suitcase is . . . than I thought. (heavy)
   e. This new chair is extremely . . . . (comfortable)
   f. Don't you have a . . . book than that? (interesting)
   g. I can't see it very . . . . (clear)
   h. You're walking very . . . today! (slow)
   i. They say that men drive . . . and . . . than women do. (fast) (reckless)

3. Use the model and write more sentences of your own using the cues:
   MODEL: He drives much more carefully now than he used to.
   CUES: sing / good
   WRITE: **She sings much better now than she used to**

Cues:
a. play / good
b. eat / slow
c. speak English / fluent
d. work / careful
e. speak / clear
f. work / hard
g. drive / careless
h. dance / bad
i. go to bed / late

4. **Guided Composition**
   Read the conversation between Joe and Susan again (page 48), and then write a conversation between a man who is lost and a policeman, using the cues:
   MAN: Excuse // get / the Central Hotel? //
   POLICEMAN: Sorry // What / say? //
   MAN: How / Central Hotel? // stranger here //
   POLICEMAN: Yes. // that street / second intersection / right // Then / until / traffic light . . .
   MAN: Traffic light?
   POLICEMAN: Yes. // When / first traffic light / right // not miss //
   MAN: very far? // how long / walk there? //
   POLICEMAN: 10 minutes / fast //
   MAN: see // Thank you //

5. **Transfer Exercise**
   Now write some true sentences about yourself or your relatives or friends. Use these models:
   I . . . much more . . .-ly than I used to.
   He . . . far . . .-er than he used to.
   Examples:
   My brother writes much better than he used to.
   I drive far more carefully than I used to.
   My sister types much faster than she used to.

1

a. When / land / on the moon?

b. stay / long?

c. When / take off?

d. astronauts / inside?

e. walk on the moon?

2

a. What / Fred / a few seconds?

b. What / yard?

c. Where / dog / now?

d. Fred's puppy / do?

3

a. What / Jane and boyfriend?

b. What / fastest way?

c. When / bus?

d. What / Jane / think?

4

a. What / Joe and Susan?

b. When / start?

c. When / guests?

d. What / Joe want to know?

5

a. Where / Bruce and Laura?

b. When / curtain?

c. What / Laura / say?

6

a. Why / Jane / get wet?

b. What / driver?

I am
He / she is
We / you / they are

going to do / go / come (etc.) if { *does*
                                      { *doesn't do*

9a

1

The spacecraft is going to land on the moon in a few seconds. It is not going to stay there very long. It is going to take off again in 24 hours. Are the astronauts going to stay inside the spacecraft? Or are they going to walk on the moon?
1. Give short answers with *is / isn't* or *are / aren't*:
    a. Is the spacecraft going to take off now?
    b. Is it going to land soon?
    c. Is it going to stay there very long?
2. Ask questions about the astronauts:
    a. inside   b. on the moon

2

Fred Collins is going to get a big shock in a few seconds. He does not know that there is a big dog in the yard and that it is hiding behind the fence. What is the dog going to do? What do you think Fred's little puppy is going to do?
1. What kind of shock is Fred going to get?
2. Ask why (and answer).
3. Ask and answer a question with *going to* about the little puppy.

3

Jane and her boyfriend saw a movie in San Francisco this evening. The fastest way home is by bus but they are obviously going to miss it. It is going to leave any second. "I'm going to find a boyfriend with a car!" Jane is thinking to herself.
Ask and answer the questions:
a. What / this evening
b. What / fastest way home
c. catch or miss
d. When / leave

4

Joe and Susan are going to give a party this evening. A lot of people are going to come. The party is going to start at 8:30, so the first guests are going to come any minute. "When are you going to take off that apron?" Joe wants to know. "In a minute," Susan answers.
1. Ask and answer the questions:
    a. When / a party
    b. start
    c. the guests
2. What is Susan doing and what is she going to do?

5

Bruce and Laura are at a concert again. The curtain is going to rise and the concert is going to begin in a few seconds. "I hope those people are going to stop laughing and talking!" Laura is saying loudly. "We aren't going to hear very well if they continue!"
1. Ask and answer the questions:
    a. When / the curtain
    b. the concert / soon
2. What does Laura hope the people in front of them are going to do and why?

6

It is going to rain and Jane doesn't have an umbrella. "I'm going to get very wet if that bus doesn't come soon!" she is saying to herself. She does not know it but the driver of that car is going to stop and he is going to offer her a ride.
1. Ask and answer the questions:
    a. raining now   b. soon
2. What is going to happen if the bus doesn't come soon?
3. What is it that Jane doesn't know?

9b FORMATION AND MANIPULATION

1 Pronunciation

REMEMBER: *going to* (in *going to* + *verb*) is often pronounced / gunna / .

For example: The spacecraft is going to (/ gunna /) land on the moon. (situation 1, page 51)

2

A	B	C	D
He's	going to	come in	soon.

a. Think of words to replace *He's* in box A.
b. Think of words to replace *come in* in box C.
c. Now write five sentences using the words you have for boxes A and C.

3 Very often when we use *going to,* we also say the time. Look at the situations on page 51 and find other time expressions to replace those in **2** box D.

4 Now look at this sentence:

A	B	C	D	E
I'm	not going to	see	him	today.

Here are some time expressions that we use with *going to*:

NOW   TOMORROW   NEXT WEEK   NEXT MONTH

a. Think of words to replace those in boxes A, C, D and E.
b. Say and write as many sentences as you can using all the words you have for exercise **a** and Part **3**.

5 Now, make questions (and answer them) using the correct parts of the table above and question words like *Where . . . ?, When . . . ?, Why . . . ?* and *How . . . ?*
Example: **When are you going to meet him? As soon as possible.**

6 *It's going to* (page 51, situation 6)
We talk about what the weather is going to do like this:
(Make sentences.)

It's going to	rain snow stop begin	soon. in a minute. in a little while. tomorrow.

7 Notice this structure from page 51, situation 6:
(Make sentences.)

I'm He's She's	going to	get wet be tired be late	if	the bus the train	doesn't	arrive. come soon. get here.

The Man Who Escaped
EPISODE 9

SUMMARY: *Driving through Kansas City, Fletcher accidentally drove by Police Headquarters. Rossi was at Police Headquarters when Wilcox found out that Fletcher was driving a 1968 blue Chevrolet truck.*

Rossi and Wilcox left Police Headquarters just in time to see Fletcher drive through the intersection. They recognized the blue truck at once.

5 Rossi jumped into the police car. Wilcox was right behind him. "Don't turn on the siren," Rossi said, as Wilcox started the engine. "I don't want him to know we're following him."

"It's ridiculous!" Wilcox said. "What kind 10 of nut is he? Does he really think he's going to escape from us if he drives right up to the front door of a police station?"

"Fletcher's no fool," Rossi answered. "In the first place, he probably had no idea he was 15 near a police station. And in the second place, he probably doesn't realize that we already know about the truck."

A few minutes later, Rossi saw the taillights of the truck.

20 "Look!" he shouted. "There he is! He's driving faster now! He probably saw us." The truck passed under a streetlight and Wilcox saw it clearly. "We've got him!" Wilcox shouted as the police car skidded around a 25 corner.

The truck turned sharply, then suddenly went up over the curb and hit a tree in front of a house.

"Stop the car!" shouted Rossi. Wilcox put 30 on the brakes. "He's not going to get away this time!" Rossi jumped out of the car and ran towards the truck. Wilcox followed right behind him. He did not take time to turn off the engine.

35 Fletcher jumped out of the truck. He started running as fast as he could toward the house. Glancing back over his shoulder, he saw two men running after him. In that instant he decided on a plan. He circled around the house, 40 and found his way back to the street. Then he ran to the police car and jumped in.

Wilcox and Rossi chased Fletcher behind the house. They were trying to decide which way to go when they heard a car engine. Suddenly 45 they both realized exactly what was happening. "He's going to get away!" shouted Rossi. They ran back just in time to see the police car disappear down the street. Fletcher was gone and so was their car!

9d FURTHER PRACTICE

1 / Invention Exercise

Ask questions with "Are(n't) you, is(n't) he, etc., going to (do) . . . ?"

CUE: Mary / tonight?
RESPONSE: **Are you going to see Mary tonight?**
or: **Isn't he going to take Mary out tonight?**
or: **Aren't you going to call Mary tonight?**

Cues:

a. a car / next week
b. the train / soon

c. television / tonight
d. a taxi

e. married / later
f. the beach / this summer

g. that letter / soon
h. a cup of coffee for me

2 / Conversation

Two years ago, before he came to San Francisco, Tom Morrison taught English in Paris. He taught at an institute for adult students. One evening he went to another institute to help give oral examinations.

TOM: You speak English very well. I'm going to give you a very good grade. Don't worry.

STUDENT (Girl): Thank you very much.

TOM: Not at all. Oh, when you go out, please tell the next student to come in.

STUDENT: Certainly. Good-bye. (Goes out, closing door. Short pause. Another person comes in)

WOMAN: Excuse me. Are you Mr. Morrison?

TOM: Yes. You don't know me, of course. I don't teach here. I just give oral examinations here now and then. Don't be nervous.

WOMAN: Nervous? Who? Me?

TOM: Sit down, please. I'm going to ask you a few questions. Then we're going to have a short conversation in English. Do you understand?

WOMAN: Of course! But I . . .

TOM: Just concentrate on my questions for the moment. First of all, why are you learning English?

WOMAN: Mr. Morrison, I don't think you understand . . .

TOM: Oh, I understand all right. I know it's important to have English to get a good job and all, but is that the *only* reason you're interested in studying English?

WOMAN: If you would listen to me for a minute! I just came in here to ask you a simple question!

TOM: (irritated) Very well. If you insist. What is it?

WOMAN: Would you like a cup of coffee?

TOM: What did you say?

WOMAN: I'm one of the teachers here. I came to ask you if you would like some coffee!

Questions

1. Why did Tom go to the institute that evening?
2. Who did he think the woman was?
3. Who was the woman really?
4. Ask and answer why she came in.

Recall

Without looking at the text, try to remember what Tom and the woman said with these words:

TOM: sit / a few questions // Then / short conversation first / why / English? // understand / important / good job / but / only reason? //

WOMAN: if / listen / minute // came / simple question // you / coffee? //

e / Summary

Focal Points in this Unit

1. Remember how we use *going to* to talk about things in the future:

		in a few seconds
a.	They're going to give a party	in a minute today (later
b.	We aren't going to watch it +	today) this evening
c.	Are you going to tell him	next week now (very) soon

2. Remember the form of the verb after *if* in sentences like:

> We aren't going to hear very well *if they continue.*
>
> I'm going to get very wet *if the bus doesn't come* soon.

f / Exercises for Homework

1. Do all the exercises on pages 51, 52 and 54.

2. Complete these sentences, using *going to* or *not going to*:

   Example:

   > I watched *World of Sports* on TV last week, but . . . (not / next week).

   You write:

   > **I watched *World of Sports* on TV last week, but I'm not going to watch it next week.**

   a. Jane caught the 7:45 bus yesterday, but . . . (not / tomorrow).

   b. I didn't see the movie last week, but . . . (next week).

   c. She bought some meat in that supermarket last Monday, but . . . (not / next time).

   d. I didn't fly the last time, but . . . (next time).

   e. We stayed at home last night, but . . . (not / tonight).

   f. I spent $50 on Christmas presents last year, but . . . (not / so much this year).

   g. They broadcast the President's speech yesterday, and . . . (again tonight).

   h. We didn't plan our vacation last summer, but . . . (this summer).

   i. I visited Bill at the hospital this morning, but . . . (not / again today).

   j. I didn't pay the bill when it came, but . . . (very soon).

3. **Guided Composition**

   Read situation 4 on page 51 again carefully. Then write a telephone conversation between Joe and one of his friends, Bill. Pretend that the conversation took place a week before the party. Try to use some of the phrases from the Conversation on page 54 too. Begin like this:

   JOE: Hello, Bill. This is Joe Freeman.

   BILL: Hello, Joe. How are you?

   JOE: I'm fine. Bill, we're going to give a party next week. Can you come?

   BILL: Sure! What day next week? And who all is going to be there?

   (Now, you continue the telephone conversation.)

4. **Transfer Exercise**

   Think about your own schedule and plans, and write 5 true sentences about things you are going to do tomorrow, the next day or next week.

1

a. How / Laura / feel?

b. What / husband / say?

c. What / Laura / want?

d. What / Bruce?

2

a. What sort of service / waiters?

b. What / Bruce order?

c. What / headwaiter?

3

a. What / Tom?

b. How / last class / room?

c. What / student?

d. Tom saying?

4

a. When / Peter / from Europe?

b. When / plane / land?

c. What / Peter / to customs officer?

d. customs officer saying?

5

a. Who / new boyfriend?

b. Where / now?

c. his question?

d. Jane's answer?

6

a. What / later?

b. the men / ask a moment ago?

c. headwaiter saying?

Shall I
Would you

take
get
bring
show

someone something?

10a

1

Laura feels terrible this morning. "Shall I bring you something to eat now?" her husband asked her a few seconds ago. "No, bring me some aspirin instead," Laura told him. Bruce is going to get her the aspirin now.

1. Ask how Laura feels this morning.
2. What exactly did her husband ask her?
3. What exactly did Laura tell him?
4. What is Bruce going to do?

2

Bruce often eats here. The waiters always give him the best service. The headwaiter spoke to Bruce only a minute ago. "Bring us some coffee now, please!" Bruce told him. The headwaiter is talking to another waiter now. "Take them some coffee!" he is saying. "Take it to them now!"

1. Ask what the waiters always do and why.
2. What did the headwaiter do and when?
3. Ask what Bruce told him (and answer).
4. What is the headwaiter saying now?

3

Tom is going to teach his class in this room, but the last class left the room in a terrible mess. A student is going to help him clean it up. "Would you close the window, please?" Tom is saying. Someone should erase the board and pick the books and chairs up too.

1. What is Tom going to do?
2. What did the last class do?
3. What is the student going to do?
4. What is Tom saying?
5. What else could he say with "Would . . . ?"

4

Joe's younger brother, Peter, flew back from Europe today. His plane landed only a few minutes ago. When the customs officer asked him if he had anything to declare, he told him he didn't. The customs officer does not believe him. "Would you show me what's in that suitcase?" he is asking.

1. What did Peter do today and when did his plane land?
2. Where is he now?
3. What did the customs officer ask him and what did Peter tell him?
4. What is the customs officer saying now?

5

This is Jane's new boyfriend. He is the one who offered her a ride a few days ago. They are at the movies now. "Shall I get you some popcorn?" he is asking. "Thanks. I'd like some," Jane replies.

1. Who is the young man with Jane and what did he do a few days ago?
2. What is he offering to get her now?
3. What exactly is he saying and what is Jane's answer?

6

There is going to be a reception in this room later. A few minutes ago none of the men knew what to do. "Where shall we put the piano?" "What shall I do with the flowers?" they asked. The headwaiter is telling them now. "Bring the flowers here and take the piano over there!" he is saying.

1. What is going to happen here later?
2. What questions did the men ask a moment ago and why?
3. What is the headwaiter saying now?

10b FORMATION AND MANIPULATION

1 Pronounciation

Shall (/ šæl /) is often pronounced / šəl / (the weak or unstressed form). Notice the way the teacher says *shall*. Now, read the following sentences aloud until you can say *shall* in its weak form correctly and without hesitation.

a. Shall I type those letters now?
b. When shall I call you?
c. Shall I get more flowers?
d. Where shall I put the flowers?
e. What shall I do with the milk?
f. Shall I answer the phone for you?

2

A	B	C
Would you	open the door,	please?

a. What other word can you put in box A to replace *Would*?
b. Look at the situations on page 57; there are many phrases there which you can put in box B.
c. Now say and / or write ten sentences beginning "Would / Could you . . . ?"

3

A	B	C	D	E
Would you	give	me	a book,	please?

a. Look at these words: GET BUY BRING SEND
   Which box can you put them in: A, B or C?
b. Think of some other words to replace *me* in box C.
c. Now, think of five things which you can put in box D.
d. Now write or say some sentences beginning with "Would / Could you . . .?"

4

A	B	C
Shall I	come in	now?

a. Look at the situations on page 57. How many words can you find to replace *come in* in box B?
   Example: **get you some popcorn**
b. Here are some more time expressions which you can use in box C:
   IN A FEW MINUTES   TOMORROW   RIGHT AWAY   RIGHT NOW
c. Make questions using the words that can go in boxes A, B and C.

5 Ask the person sitting next to you questions with "Would / Could you . . . ?" and "Shall I . . . ?" using the following cues:

open the window	show me / him the book	phone me / you later	give me / her a drink of water
turn on the radio	ask them to come in	make me / them a cake	get me / her a newspaper

The answers to these questions can be:
Yes, of course or *Certainly* or *I'm sorry, but I can't at the moment.*

The Man Who Escaped
EPISODE 10

SUMMARY: Rossi and Wilcox jumped in a police car and followed Fletcher's truck for several miles. Finally, Fletcher's truck went off the road and hit a tree in front of a house. Rossi and Wilcox ran after Fletcher, but Fletcher circled around the house and drove off in their police car.

Fletcher finally remembered who the man was. "Rossi of the FBI! Of course!" Fletcher said to himself. He slowed down so he would not attract attention. He felt nervous in the
5 police car and he wanted to get rid of it.
"I wonder how they found out about the truck . . . ?" he asked himself. Then he remembered the police car he saw on the Leavenworth road near the farm and the
10 policeman who tried to stop him.
"That's the answer!" he thought." That policeman was on his way to the farm. Somebody finally helped him. He went to the farmhouse . . . and then he radioed the police."
15 Suddenly he saw lights on the road ahead of him. Two police cars were parked across the road. It was a roadblock!

The two policemen at the roadblock were shivering in the cold night air.
20 "Give me a light, will you?" one of them said. The other policeman held out his lighter. Just then they saw headlights approaching.
"It's a police car," one of them said. "Do you think they're bringing us some hot cof-
25 fee?" They both watched as the car came closer. It was coming very fast.
"Isn't he going to stop?"
"It doesn't look like it."
"Shall we stop him? Our orders are not to let
30 anybody through."
Then they heard the siren. It was obvious that the police car was not going to stop.

The two policemen hesitated for an instant. Then both men jumped into their cars and
35 quickly moved them off the road. They watched as Fletcher raced past them.

After going through the roadblock, Fletcher knew that he had to act fast. Soon there would be police cars everywhere. The railroad yards
40 were just a few miles ahead. "I'll jump on a freight train!" he decided. "That will be the safest way to get out of Kansas City and to get to Chicago to look for Kincaid and Hooper."

10d FURTHER PRACTICE

1 / Invention Exercise

Ask questions with "Shall I . . . ?" or "Would you
. . . ?" using the cues. Make 2 sentences from the cues
when you can.

CUE: those books
RESPONSE: **Shall I carry those books for you?**
or: **Would you carry those books for me?**

Cues:

a. the windows
b. that letter
c. the grass
d. a cup of tea
e. your breakfast
f. your suitcase
g. the light
h. the radio
i. time
j. more clearly / slowly

2 / Conversation

Bruce often travels to other places. This is a typical
conversation at the front desk of a hotel.

DESK CLERK: Good evening, sir.

BRUCE: Good evening. My name's Foster. I have a
reservation.

CLERK: Just a moment, Mr. Foster. Let's see . . .
Foster . . . yes, Mr. Foster, room 204. Would you
register, please?

BRUCE: All right. Uh . . . I can't find my pen and there
isn't one on the desk.

CLERK: Oh! No, there isn't. That's strange.

BRUCE: Maybe someone walked off with it. Could you
lend me yours?

CLERK: Of course. Here you are. How long are you
going to stay, Mr. Foster?

BRUCE: I'm not sure. It all depends. But I'm probably
going to leave on Thursday.

CLERK: On Thursday. All right. Would you tell us as
soon as you know for sure?

BRUCE: Yes. I'll be using a credit card. Would you like
it now?

CLERK: No, that's not necessary, Mr. Foster.

BRUCE: Oh, would you call me at 7 in the morning?

CLERK: At 7. Sure. Front desk! (to bellman) Take Mr.
Foster's bags to his room. Just follow the bellman,
Mr. Foster.

BRUCE: Thank you.

CLERK: Oh! Excuse me, Mr. Foster. My pen!

BRUCE: Your pen?

CLERK: Yes. I lent it to you a moment ago. Remember?

BRUCE: Oh, I'm sorry. I put it in my pocket by
mistake. Here you are.

CLERK: Thank you.

Questions

1. What is the first thing Bruce says when he goes into
   the hotel?
2. What is the next thing Bruce has to do?
3. How exactly does the clerk ask him to do this?
4. What does the desk clerk do when Bruce tells him
   there isn't a pen on the counter?
5. How does Bruce ask him to do this?
6. What does Bruce say when the clerk asks how long
   he is going to stay?
7. When does Bruce want to get up and what does he
   say about this?

Correct the statements

1. Bruce lent the desk clerk his pen.
2. He is sure he is going to leave on Thursday.
3. Bruce intended to put the pen in his pocket.

Practice

Practice the intonation of *Would you . . . ?, Sure* and
Remember? (Don't you remember?).

e / Summary

Focal Points in this Unit

1. Remember the polite way we ask other people to do things for us:

   Would you
   Could you   open the window, please?

2. Remember how we offer to do something:
   Shall I carry that for you?
   Shall I get you some popcorn?

3. With words like *give, bring, take, get, show, send* and *lend* in the table below, use this word order:

1	2	3
Shall I send Could you give	him her them	some money? the books? the letter?

Notice particularly the form of the words in column 2.

f / Exercises for Homework

1. Do all the questions and exercises on pages 57 and 60.

2. Choose the correct form:
   a. Shall I mail that letter . . . ? (your / you / for you)
   b. Would you give . . . the book, please? (to me / me / I)
   c. Could you lend . . . some money? (him / he / to him)
   d. Shall I take . . . a gift when I go to see her? (she / to her / her)
   e. Would you give . . . these letters, please? (them / to them / they)

3. Put the words in their correct order to make sentences:
   Example:
   to read / Joe / a book / going / is

Answer: **Joe is going to read a book.**
   a. bring / I / you / a cup of coffee / shall?
   b. that phone / you / could / for me / answer?
   c. your address / me / could / give / you?
   d. me / yesterday / sent / a package / my parents.
   e. five dollars / them / last night / lent / he.

4. **Guided Composition**
   You got back from your vacation yesterday. Before you went on vacation, you left a book at a friend's house, and you want him / her to bring it back as soon as possible. Write a letter asking for it. Begin your letter like this:

   > Dear . . .,
   >   I flew back from Mexico last night after a wonderful vacation. When I came through customs, . . .

   Now continue the letter using as many of the following cue words and phrases as you can, and any other words and phrases from this unit (particularly pages 57 and 60):

   > Customs officer / anything to declare // "show / suitcase" // no money / people / offer / ride // kind of them // more about vacation / see you // remember / book / your house? // bring / next week? //

5. **Transfer Exercise**
   a. Write down what you say if you want someone (1) to give you a bag for your groceries, (2) to tell you the time, (3) to carry something for you, (4) to answer the phone (or front door), and (5) to lend you a particular book.
   b. Write down what you say when you offer (1) to open a window, (2) to close a door, (3) to help someone, (4) to put something somewhere, and (5) to sign a document (sales contract, check, letter, etc.).

1

a. When / boyfriend?

b. When / Jane?

c. What time / now?

d. Why / he / upset?

2

a. How long / Joe and Susan?

b. How long / house?

c. How long / the Barclays?

d. How long / their house?

3

a. How long / Peter / in the country?

b. When / woman?

c. How long / Peter / wait?

d. How long / woman / talk?

4

a. How long / Jane / office?

b. How long / others / work?

c. What / typists?

5

a. How long / game?

b. When / game / start?

c. What / police?

d. What / TV camera?

e. Why / Joe / better view?

Has / Have had
Has / Have been
Has / Have been doing

for 10 minutes / 6 months / 3 years

since 9 o'clock / 1975 / last Friday

11a

1

Jane had a date with her new boyfriend in this restaurant at 8:00. He came on time but she did not. She came in only a moment ago. It is 9 o'clock. "Have you been waiting long?" she asked him when she came in. "Yes, I have," he is saying. He is a little upset because he has been waiting for an hour.

1. Ask when he came. Ask about Jane too.
2. What exactly is her question?
3. What exactly is his answer?
4. Why is he upset?

2

Joe and Susan have been married a very short time. They haven't had this house very long. The couple next door, the Barclays, have been married a very long time. They have been living in the same house for many years!

Ask questions with *very long*:
a. Joe and Susan / married
b. the Barclays / married
c. Joe and Susan / that house

3

Joe's brother, Peter, has been back in the country for only half an hour. He is waiting to call Joe, but some woman got to the phone booth just a few seconds before he did. That was ten minutes ago. She has been talking for ten minutes and Peter has been waiting that long too.

Ask and answer questions with *How long*:
a. Peter / back in the country
b. woman / in the phone booth
c. Peter / outside
d. talk
e. wait

4

Jane has been working in the office since 8:30. The others haven't. They have only been there for ten minutes. They have been in the office since 9 o'clock. Actually one man has been standing by the window for the last ten minutes. The two typists have not been doing very much either. They have been talking.

1. Say what each person is doing now.
2. Now ask questions with *How long*.
3. Make sentences with *since* and *for*.

5

This game has been going on for half an hour. The teams have only been playing since 2:30 and there is trouble already. In the very first minute, some of the crowd began to throw things and fight. The stadium police have been trying to keep order and have been talking to people in the grandstand. A TV camera has been filming everything. There is a very tall man in front of Joe. Joe has been trying to get a better view for some time, but it is impossible.

1. Ask and answer questions with *How long*:
   a. the game   d. the police
   b. the teams   e. a TV camera
   c. some of the crowd   f. Joe / a better view
2. Make sentences with *since* and *for* about all the things you see in the picture.

11b FORMATION AND MANIPULATION

1 Pronunciation

a. *I've* is more frequent than *I have* in constructions such as *I've called, I've been there,* etc. Notice the contractions *I've, you've, she's, he's, we've, they've.*

b. *For* is almost always pronounced / f ə r / .

2

A	B	C
I've	been living in Boston	for ages.

a. Think of all the other words that can replace *I've* in box A.

b. Now look at the situations on page 63 and find words to replace *been living in Boston* in box B.

c. Look at the situations on page 63 again. This time find all the time expressions that can replace *for ages* in box C.

d. Now, write or say ten sentences using the words that can go in boxes A, B and C.

e. The word *had* can also go in box B if you put words like *a car, a big house* after it.

f. Make five sentences with "I've (etc.) had a . . ."

3

A	B	C	D
How long	has he	been living	in Boston?

a. Think of all the words which can replace *has he* in box B.

b. Now replace boxes C and D (refer to the situations on page 63).

c. Look at these time expressions; some you know, some are new:

FOR AGES   SINCE LAST SUMMER   FOR A WEEK   SINCE CHRISTMAS   FOR A VERY LONG TIME
SINCE YESTERDAY   FOR YEARS AND YEARS   SINCE 1974   FOR A MINUTE   SINCE HE ARRIVED

d. Use the expressions in exercise **c** to answer questions beginning with *How long.* Ask and answer these questions with the person sitting next to you.

   Example: A: **How long have you been living here?**

   B: **Since last summer.**

4

A	B	C
Have you	been in the U.S.	very long?

a. Look at these words; they can replace *been in the U.S.* in box B:

   known him   had a cold   been waiting for them

b. With the person sitting next to you, ask and answer questions with *very long.* For affirmative answers use *Yes* plus the time expression in Part **3,** exercise **c.** For negative answers use the *No, not very long* or *No, I haven't* forms.

The Man Who Escaped
EPISODE 11

SUMMARY: *Fletcher was driving in the stolen police car when he finally remembered that the man he saw was Richard Rossi of the FBI. He wanted to get rid of the police car. Suddenly he saw a roadblock ahead of him, but he went through it without stopping. He decided to go to the railroad yards and get on a freight train leaving Kansas City.*

Rossi was angry. He and Wilcox were waiting for a police car to come and pick them up. They had been waiting for a long time because most of the policemen were busy setting up roadblocks.

Rossi was angry because Fletcher got away. He could imagine what Howard Becker, his chief, would say. "Well, Rossi," he would say sarcastically, "it wasn't very nice of Fletcher to take your car, was it? But at least you were kind enough to leave the motor running for him!"

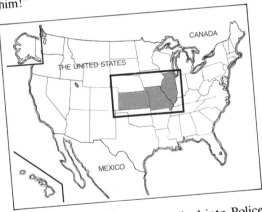

When Rossi and Wilcox walked into Police Headquarters, the desk sergeant called to Wilcox. "Lieutenant! We've got something!" He was holding the phone and writing notes with his other hand. "We got a report about a police car that drove through a roadblock. And I've been talking to Sergeant Miller of the 3rd Precinct. His men found a car near the railroad yards. It looks like one of ours!"

"It must be the one I was driving," said Wilcox.

In his apartment in Chicago, John Kincaid was listening to the news. Fletcher was still free. Kincaid frowned. He turned off the radio and reached for the telephone.

Rossi and Wilcox parked in front of the railroad station. A police officer was standing by the door of the freight office. He pointed to the office. "The stationmaster's in there. Officer O'Malley's been talking to him for five or ten minutes."

Inside, O'Malley explained that he questioned everybody, but nobody knew anything

about the police car. Rossi was not interested in the police car, however. He was thinking of something else. He wanted to know about train schedules.

"A freight train to St. Louis left about an hour ago," the stationmaster said. Rossi explained that the man they were looking for was probably on that train. "We want to search the train at one of its stops before it gets to St. Louis," he said.

"If you can get there in time," the stationmaster said, "the first stop is Jefferson City. Maybe you could get a helicopter . . ."

11d FURTHER PRACTICE

1 / Conversation for Paired Practice

Read the model conversation, and use the cues to make others like it.

MODEL: A: **Are you still living in Boston?**
         B: **Yes, I've been living there for three years now.**

Cues:

a. A: working for them
   B: two years

b. A: taking swimming lessons
   B: a couple of months

c. A: studying English
   B: eighteen months

d. A: reading that book
   B: six weeks

e. A: writing that letter
   B: half an hour

f. A: waiting to see the boss
   B: ages

2 / Conversation

Two months ago Jane bought a sweater from a large department store. The sweater is coming apart already. Jane took the sweater back during her lunch hour today. She went there with a friend, Mary, who works in the same office. This is what happened.

MARY: It's certainly very busy here today, isn't it?

JANE: Yes, and there aren't enough salespeople. We've been standing here for at least five minutes!

MARY: Quick. Catch that girl's eye! She's just finishing with a customer.

JANE: Miss! Miss! Excuse me. I think I'm next and I don't have very much time.

SALESGIRL: Yes . . . can I help you?

JANE: Yes, I'd like to return this sweater. I've only had it for four weeks and it's coming apart.

SALESGIRL: Coming apart? May I see it?

JANE: Yes, here you are. Look at the sleeves. They're the worst. See? They're coming apart.

SALESGIRL: And how long did you say you've had it?

JANE: For only four weeks. Since Christmas, in fact. Look, here's the sales slip.

SALESGIRL: Thank you. This is very strange. We've been selling this particular kind for years and we haven't had any complaints in all that time.

JANE: Well, I'm sorry. I'm sure it isn't my fault that it's not holding up.

SALESGIRL: One moment, please. Let me call the manager. Mr. Simons! Mr. Simons!

MR. SIMONS: Yes?

SALESGIRL: This lady's had this sweater for four weeks and it's falling apart.

MR. SIMONS: Really? Let me see it, please. Hmmm . . . yes . . .

JANE: I've been wearing it on weekends; that's all.

MR. SIMONS: Yes, well . . . make out a credit slip for her, would you, Miss Smith?

JANE: I'd rather have my money back, if you don't mind.

MR. SIMONS: I see. Well, I suppose we can arrange that.

JANE: Thank you.

Correct the statements

1. There are not many people in the store today.
2. Jane has a lot of time.
3. She has been standing there for an hour.
4. She has had the sweater for a year.
5. The store hasn't been selling that particular kind for long.
6. Jane has been wearing the sweater to work.
7. Jane wants a credit slip for the sweater.

Answer these questions

1. Ask and answer how long Jane has been standing there.
2. Ask why.
3. Why isn't she satisfied with the sweater?
4. What exactly does she say when the manager offers her a credit slip?

Practice

Think of some more sentences of your own using the pattern *I'd rather . . ., if you don't mind.* Describe the situations we can use these sentences in.

e / Summary

Focal Points in this Unit

1. a. Look at the ideas which are expressed in a *have been* sentence:

I am in Boston. I have been in
I came here 3 Boston for
years ago. 3 years.

b. Now look at a *have had* sentence:

I have a car. I have had a car
I bought it 6 for 6 months.
months ago.

c. Now look at a *have been (do)ing* sentence:

It is snowing. It has been snow-
It started snowing ing for an hour.
an hour ago.

2. To ask questions about a period of time, we use the form:

How long + have been doing . . .?
 have had . . .?

Examples:

How long have you been studying English?
How long have you had that car?

3. Remember that *since* is used with times that we can point to on a calendar or clock.

since + 6 o'clock / yesterday
 last Monday / last January
 March 15 / 1975 / Easter

Since is also used with phrases to which the speaker can put a definite time or date.

since + the end of the war / I was 6
 I left school / she got married
 his last birthday
 the last office party

4. Remember that *for* is used with periods of time.

for + half an hour / 45 minutes
 3 hours / 2 days / 6 weeks
 2 weeks / 18 months
 25 years / ages and ages
 a week or so

f / Exercises for Homework

1. Do all the exercises and questions on pages 63, 64 and 66.

2. Invention Exercise
With *has / have been doing . . . for / since*
Examples:
a. CUE: work / Dallas / 2 years
 RESPONSE: **I've been working in Dallas for 2 years.**
b. CUE: live / Detroit / 1974
 RESPONSE: **She's been living in Detroit since 1974.**
Cues:
a. wait / bus / 10 minutes
b. study / English / 6 months
c. work / yard / 1 o'clock
d. travel / all the time / 2 years
e. drive / that car / 3 years
f. live / an apartment / last July
g. build / that house / March
h. look for / prisoner / he escaped
i. ring / doorbell / 5 minutes

3. Guided Composition
Write a letter to a store about an orlon sweater you bought while you were on vacation in New York about a month ago. You want to return it because it is coming apart. Read the Conversation on page 66 again, and try to use as many words, phrases and patterns as you can in your letter. These patterns are particularly useful: *I'd like to return this sweater / . . . it's already falling apart / it isn't my fault . . . / I'd rather . . ., if you don't mind.* Begin your letter like this:
Dear Sir:
 While I was on vacation in New York about a month ago, I bought a green orlon sweater in your store. I'm afraid . . .

4. Transfer Exercise
Write 10 true sentences about yourself or friends using *have done, have been,* or *have been doing* + *since* or *for.*
Examples:
I've had this car for 3 years.

I've been studying English since 1976.

1

a. How long / they / club?

b. What time?

c. good time?

d. What / Laura / say?

e. Where / other people?

2

a. Fred / wife / good time?

b. Where / the children?

c. Why / quiet?

3

a. Where / Jane?

b. How long / bus?

c. What / around corner?

4

a. What / Peter?

b. How long?

c. What / operator?

d. Why / Peter / hang up?

5

a. Who / Peter / stay with?

b. How long / job?

c. What / Joe / tell / Peter?

6

a. How / Frank / lately?

b. Why / overtime?

c. What / doctor / say?

Present Perfect Continuous (continued)
Present Perfect + *just* and *yet*
Had better do and *Had better not do*

12a

1

Bruce and Laura have been in a nightclub since 8 p.m.
It is 2 in the morning now. They have been having a
very good time. "I really think we'd better leave
now," Laura is telling Bruce. "Everybody else has
gone home except the waiters and the band."
1. Ask and answer the questions:
   a. Where / now   c. What time / now
   b. How long   d. a good time
2. What is Laura telling Bruce?
3. Do you agree? Why?

2

Fred Collins and his wife have been having a good
time too. They have just come home. The children are
asleep upstairs. They had better be very quiet. They
had better look where they are going. The baby is
going to cry if they wake her up.
1. What have Fred and his wife been doing?
2. What have they just done?
3. What is going to happen if they are not careful?
4. Make some sentences about them with *had better*
   and *had better not.*

3

Jane is going to meet her boyfriend. She has been
waiting for the bus for some time but it has not come
yet. She is going to be late again if it does not come
soon. A taxi has just come around the corner. Perhaps
she had better take it.
1. What is Jane going to do?
2. What is she doing now? Ask *how long.*
3. What is going to happen if the bus does not come
   soon?
4. What has just happened?
5. What had she better do?

4

Peter is making a long distance call to Florida. He has
been talking for three minutes and the operator has
just asked him to signal her when he is through. He
doesn't have any more change. "I'm sorry," he is
saying to his friend in Florida. "I think I'd better hang
up now."
1. What is Peter doing?
2. Ask how long (and answer).
3. What has the operator just asked him to do?
4. What is he saying?

5

Peter came back to the States a month ago. He has
been staying with Joe and Susan since then. He has
been looking for a job for a month but has not found
one yet. "Some employers don't like people with long
hair," Joe is telling him. "Maybe you'd better get a
haircut!"
1. Ask and answer questions about Peter:
   a. When / back to the States
   b. How long / with Joe and Susan
   c. How long / a job
   d. one yet
2. What is Joe telling him?

6

Frank Martin has not been feeling very well lately. He
has been putting in a lot of overtime because he wants
to buy a new car. The doctor has been examining him.
"You've been working too hard, that's all," he is
saying. "You'd better slow down a little. You'd better
not work so hard."
1. What has the doctor been doing?
2. What had Frank better do and why?
3. Ask and answer the questions:
   a. very well lately
   b. Why / so much overtime lately

12b FORMATION AND MANIPULATION

1

A	B	C
He's been	having a good time.	

a. Find other words to replace *He's been* in box A.
b. Look at the situations on page 69 and find things to put in box B.
c. Box C is empty. Words like *recently* and *lately* can go here and so can expressions of time with the words *since* and *for*. Think of as many as you can. If you can't think of very many, look at the Formation and Manipulation page of Unit 11.
d. With the person sitting next to you, ask and answer questions like this:
Question: **What's he been doing recently**?
Answer: **Having a good time.** or **He's been having a good time.**
e. Now make questions starting "Have you . . .?" (answer *Yes, I have* or *No, I haven't*).
Example: Question: **Have you been having a good time recently?**
Answer: **Yes, I have.**

2 Look at these words: LOOKING   FEELING   EATING
a. Now look at the first sentence of situation 6, page 69.
b. Find other words to replace *Frank Martin, feeling* and *lately*.
c. With the person sitting next to you, ask and answer questions like this:
Question: **What's the matter with Frank Martin?**
Answer: **Oh, he hasn't been feeling very well lately.**
and like this:
Question: **What's the matter?**
Answer: **Well, actually, I haven't been feeling well lately.**

3

A	B	C	D	E
Has he	come in	yet?	Yes, he's just	come in.

a. Think of words to replace *he* in boxes A and D.
b. Now, think of words to replace *come in* in boxes B and E.
c. Now say or write five sentences using the new words you have.

4 a. Make sentences from the table.

You'd better We'd better I'd better	get some rest. go now. find a taxi.

b. Make sentences from the table.

You'd better not He'd better not They'd better not	work so hard. eat so much. go out so much.

NOTE: *'d better* is a short form of *had better*. For example: You'd better get a haircut (page 69, situation 5). Notice the contractions *I'd, you'd, she'd, he'd, we'd, they'd.*

The Man Who Escaped
EPISODE 12

SUMMARY: *Fletcher drove off in Wilcox's police car. When they got back to headquarters, the desk sergeant told them a police car had gone through a roadblock and that policemen from the 3rd Precinct had found the car at the railroad yards. Rossi thought Fletcher probably got on a freight train for St. Louis, so he made plans to search the train when it stopped in Jefferson City.*

Fletcher woke up suddenly. For a moment he did not know where he was. Then he remembered. He was on a freight train. Cautiously, he pushed the door of the boxcar
5 open and looked out. "A few more hours and we'll be in St. Louis!" he thought to himself. "Jefferson City will be the next stop, and . . .," Then he had a terrible thought. "When they find the police car, . . . they'll know how I got
10 away! Rossi is pretty smart, so he probably checked the train schedules. That means he'll be waiting for me in St. Louis . . . or . . . before that! What about Jefferson City? Of course!"

Fletcher jumped off the train before it
15 reached Jefferson City. As the train disappeared down the track, he got up from the ground and brushed the wet snow off his clothes. He walked along the tracks until he came to a highway. There was an all-night
20 diner near the highway and there were a lot of trucks parked there.

"I'm going to St. Louis, if that's any help to you," one of the truck drivers said as he pointed to his big truck. Fletcher was standing
25 near the truck in front of the diner. He wanted a cup of hot coffee, but he knew he'd better not go in.

"Thanks!" answered Fletcher. "That's exactly where I'm going," and he got in the
30 truck. As they drove through Jefferson City, he asked himself, "Do you suppose the police have searched that train yet?"

It was a little before daybreak when Fletcher arrived in St. Louis. He hurried across 7th
35 Boulevard and climbed the steps to the front door of the Hawthorne Apartments. He rang the bell for Apartment 412 several times. Finally a woman's voice came over the intercom. "Yes . . . ? Who is it . . . ?"
40 Fletcher hesitated for a moment and then said in a low voice, "Marilyn . . . ?" The intercom was quiet for a few seconds, and then the voice replied, "Gordon . . . ? Is that you?"

12d FURTHER PRACTICE

1 / Invention Exercise

Make sentences with *'d better*, using the cues.

CUE: those shoes
RESPONSE: **You'd (He'd / I'd, etc.) better polish those shoes.**
CUE: up early tomorrow
RESPONSE: **I'd better get up early tomorrow.**

Cues:

a. a haircut
b. very quiet
c. that old car
d. the bank
e. less coffee
f. bed early tonight

g. that letter now
h. a new car
i. the office earlier
j. more slowly
k. faster
l. a phone call

Describe the situations in which the sentences are used.

2 / Conversation

Frank Martin went to see his doctor last week, but he was not satisfied with what the doctor told him. He asked to see a specialist. This is what happened when he saw Dr. Scott, the specialist.

DR. SCOTT: Now, Mr. Martin, I've just been reading what your own doctor says. I gather you haven't been feeling very well lately. Is that right?

FRANK: It's . . . it's my leg, Doctor. My right leg. I keep getting a strange pain in it.

DR. SCOTT: Could you describe this pain to me?

FRANK: It's like . . . like boiling water running down my leg. It's been getting worse lately too. I haven't been sleeping well at all.

DR. SCOTT: You mean the pain's been keeping you awake?

FRANK: Yes. It's been keeping me awake almost every night.

DR. SCOTT: Now, tell me, how long have you had this trouble?

FRANK: The pain? For about a year now.

DR. SCOTT: Hmmm . . . Have you been getting especially tired lately after walking short distances? For instance, have you been getting a bit short of breath, maybe?

FRANK: Yes! Yes, I have!

DR. SCOTT: Hmmm . . . I think we'd better give you a few tests here in the hospital.

FRANK: Do you think it's anything serious, Doctor?

DR. SCOTT: Probably not.

FRANK: But . . . Doctor Cook, my family doctor, thinks it's only that I've been working too hard lately.

DR. SCOTT: That could be the reason. Don't worry. We'll soon find out.

Correct the statements

1. Frank has been getting a strange pain in his arm.
2. It has been getting better lately.
3. Frank's own doctor thinks he has been eating too much lately.
4. The specialist thinks that Dr. Cook is mistaken in his diagnosis.

Questions

1. What has the pain been doing to Frank?
2. What has been happening to Frank after he has taken short walks?
3. What does the specialist think they had better do?

Ask and answer the questions about Frank

1. How long / this trouble?
2. pain / better or worse lately?

e / Summary

Focal Points in this Unit

1. Remember how we use the words *just* and *yet* with the Present Perfect:
   a. He has *just* come home. / A taxi has *just* come around the corner. / The operator has *just* asked him to signal when he is through.
   b. The bus has not come *yet*. / He has not found a job *yet*.

   Notice the position of *just* and *yet* in these sentences.

   NOTE: Remember that we also use the word *just* (but not the word *yet*) with the Simple Past tense:

   He *just* came home. / A taxi *just* came around the corner. / The operator *just* asked him to signal when he is through.

2. Remember how we use *'d better* to give advice to other people (You *'d better not work* so hard.) and to suggest that it is a good idea to do something (We *'d better leave* now. / I *'d better not tell* them.). Notice particularly the form of the verb after *had better*, and the position of *not* in negative sentences.

f / Exercises for Homework

1. Do all the questions and exercises on pages 69 and 72.

2. **Invention Exercise**
   Write sentences using the cues:

   MODEL: I've been . . . for . . ., but I haven't . . .
   since

   yet.

   Examples:
   a.   CUE: job / three weeks
      RESPONSE: **I've been looking for a job for three weeks, but I haven't found one yet.**
   b.   CUE: the bus / 9 o'clock
      RESPONSE: **I've been waiting for the bus since 9 o'clock, but it hasn't come yet.**

   Cues:
   a. my homework / half an hour
   b. the train / twenty minutes
   c. the concert / 7:30
   d. a car / 20 years
   e. the mailman / 10 o'clock
   f. this book / 2 weeks
   g. English / 18 months
   h. this letter / 6 o'clock
   i. a sports car / last Christmas
   j. records / 20 minutes

3. **Guided Composition**
   Using some of the vocabulary and sentence patterns from situation 6 (page 69) and from the Conversation (page 72), write a short letter to a friend in the Sierra Club politely refusing an invitation to go camping in the woods. Begin your letter like this:
   Dear . . .,
      Thank you very much for your invitation to go camping next weekend. It was very nice of you to think of me, but I'm afraid . . .

4. **Transfer Exercise**
   Write at least 5 sentences about yourself using this pattern:
   I haven't done the job yet, so I'd better get started right away.

   I haven't reserved seats for the concert yet, so I'd better reserve them this afternoon.

1

a. What / people / doing?

b. first time?

c. What / director?

d. What / all the different people?

e. When / "cut" / last time?

f. What / the different people / then?

2

a. What / all the people/ outlaws walked in?
(ask two questions about each person)

3

a. What / in a few seconds?

b. What / Frank / now?

c. some of the men?

d. old man?

e. manager?

f. What / manager / bell rings?

4

a. What / woman?

b. What / two old men?

c. What / young man?

d. What / children?

e. What / young couple?

He / she · was doing
We / you / they · were doing · } .... when .... *did*
He (etc.) · *did*

13a

1

These people are making a film. This is the second time they have filmed this scene. The director is going to shout "cut" in a second. Two men are fighting. The King is talking to the Queen. She is listening. A beautiful girl is crying. Two other men are watching the fight. One of them is laughing. The director shouted "cut" at exactly this point before. They were all doing the same thing when he did this. They all stopped and had a short rest when he shouted "cut."

1. Ask what these people are doing now and answer:
   a. the two men   d. the beautiful girl
   b. the King   e. the two other men
   c. the Queen
2. Now say what all these people were doing when the director shouted "cut" at this point before. Make at least five different sentences.
3. What did they all do when the director shouted "cut" last time? (short rest)

2

This is a scene from one of Felix Mendoza's very old films. It was called "The Fastest Gun in the West." Felix played the one-eyed leader of a gang of outlaws. Everybody was working in the Oak Creek Bank when Felix and his gang strolled into the bank. The cashier was counting money. The bookkeeper was making some entries in the record books. The owner of the bank was putting some money in the safe and the teller was talking to a customer. A second later, one of Felix's outlaws shouted, "This is a holdup!" and everybody stood still and raised their arms in the air.

1. Ask what each person was doing when Felix and his band of outlaws entered the bank (and answer):
   a. bookkeeper   c. cashier
   b. teller   d. owner
2. What did they all do when one of the outlaws shouted, "This is a holdup!"?

3

This is where Frank works. You can see exactly the same thing every day at this time. A bell is going to ring in a few seconds and everybody is going to rush out, as they always do. Frank is working at his machine. Some of the men are watching the clock. An old man is sweeping the floor and the factory manager is standing in front of his office. He is looking at his watch and at the men. He always goes back into his office when the bell rings. This is exactly what was happening when the bell rang yesterday too.

1. Notice the question: *Was Frank working when the bell rang yesterday?*
   Notice the short answers using the same model: *Yes, he was. / No, he wasn't.*
2. Now ask what these people were doing when the bell rang (and answer):
   a. Frank / the clock?
   b. manager / his watch?
   c. old man / the floor?
   d. some of the men / clock?

4

These two pictures show what was happening in a park yesterday afternoon and what happened in the same park a little later when it suddenly began to rain. An elderly woman was feeding some pigeons. Two old men were sitting on a park bench talking. A young man was looking at the flowers. A boy and girl were walking hand in hand. Some children were playing on the swings. When it began to rain, the two old men got up and stood under a tree. The woman put a newspaper over her head and the young man put his umbrella up. The young couple and the children began to run as fast as they could.

1. What do these two pictures show? What happened suddenly?
2. Ask questions about these people with "What was / were . . . doing before it began to rain?"
3. Now ask "What did . . . do when it began to rain?"

13b FORMATION AND MANIPULATION

1 Pronunciation

Was and *were* are words that have weak or unstressed forms which are used very frequently in spoken English.
We write: *I was there* and *We were there.*
But we say: / ay-w'z / *there* and / wiy-w'r / *there.*

2

A	B	C	D	E
She	was working	when	he	arrived.

a. Think of other words to replace *she* and *he* in boxes A and D. Don't forget that you can also use names in these boxes.

b. Read the situations on page 75 again and look for verbs to replace *work* and *arrive* in boxes B and E.

c. Now write or say ten sentences using the new words you have for the boxes.

d. Here are some more words which you can use to make sentences like *She was working when he arrived:*

B
eating breakfast
taking a bath
doing the dishes
writing a letter
making coffee
watching television
giving the baby a bath

D and E
the phone rang.
Joe arrived.
the light went out.
someone knocked at the door.
the man left.
the clock stopped.
the TV program started.
the house caught fire.
the storm hit.

e. Now, with the words in the boxes in exercise **d,** ask and answer questions like this:
Question: **What were you doing when the phone rang?**
Answer: **(I was) watching television.**

3

A	B	C	D	E
I	stood up	when	Bill	came in.

a. Look at situations 2 and 4 on page 75; you will find many verbs to replace those in boxes B and E.

b. Use those and these below to make ten new sentences like *I stood up when Bill came in:*

B
stood up
stopped talking
went away
sat down
opened the door
smiled

E
Bill came in.
the policeman left.
the doctor came in.
the music stopped.

c. Now, with the person sitting next to you, ask questions using the items in box E and answer them with the items in box B:
Example: Question: **What did you do when the policeman left?**
Answer: **(I) sat down.**

The Man Who Escaped
EPISODE 13

SUMMARY: *Fletcher got on a freight train going to St. Louis. However, he thought that the police might search the train in Jefferson City, so he jumped off before it got there. A truck driver gave him a ride and he got to St. Louis at daybreak. He went to an apartment house on 7th Boulevard. When he rang Apartment 412, a woman answered and immediately recognized his voice.*

John Kincaid was a very worried man. His hand was shaking when he picked up the phone and dialed. He waited nervously. Finally a voice answered, "Yes . . . ! Who is it . . . ?"
5 The voice sounded sleepy.

"Hooper . . . ? This is John!" Kincaid said quickly.

The man at the other end was angry.
10 "What's the matter with you, Kincaid? Why are you calling me at this hour? Do you have any idea what time it is?"

"Hooper, wait! I've got a good reason. They haven't caught Fletcher yet! He's still
15 free . . . !"

"I know that!" the man answered coldly.

"I can't sleep, Hooper! I've been thinking about Fletcher all night!" Then Kincaid almost screamed into the phone, "What are you going
20 to do about it, Hooper? What are you going to do . . . ?"

Hooper answered calmly, "What do you think we're going to do? We're going to kill him!"

25 "You're helping a man who escaped from prison," Fletcher said. They were getting into the car. "You could get into a lot of trouble, you know." The young woman looked at Fletcher and smiled, but said nothing.

30 "Everybody thinks I'm a dangerous spy," Fletcher continued.

"But *I* don't think so," she said finally.

Fletcher was silent for a few minutes. Then he said, "You're the only person who believed I
35 was innocent. That's why I asked you for help."

"But you won't tell me how I can help you!" she said. "Oh sure, I'll drive you to Chicago. But then what . . . ? What's in Chicago? What's
40 this all about? Tell me what I can do!"

Fletcher hesitated for a minute. "You can help me find the real spies," he answered slowly.

13d FURTHER PRACTICE

1 / Practice Situations

Make 2 sentences for each of these situations, one
with *was doing . . . when . . . did* and one with
did . . . when . . . did.

EXAMPLE SITUATION:
Robert drove to New Orleans yesterday. Halfway
there the car broke down. Robert walked to a garage to
get a mechanic.

EXAMPLE SENTENCES:
1. **Robert was driving to New Orleans yesterday when
   his car broke down.**
2. **When his car broke down, Robert walked to a garage
   to get a mechanic.**

Situations:

a. Jane watched a program on television last night.
   The phone rang in the middle of the program. She
   answered it.
b. Bruce dictated a letter to his secretary yesterday
   afternoon. Halfway through the letter he received a
   telephone call. He left the office immediately.
c. Laura went to a movie yesterday afternoon. In the
   middle of the main feature, the projector broke
   down. She went home.
d. The policeman walked down Main Street yesterday
   morning. A man asked him the time. The policeman
   told him.

2 / Conversation

Joe Freeman saw an accident involving two cars last
month. He is a witness in court today. You are going
to hear the lawyer for one of the drivers, then Joe, and
then the lawyer for the other driver.

1ST LAWYER: Mr. Freeman, would you please tell the
court what you were doing when the accident
happened and what you saw?
JOE: Yes, I was driving home from work. It was about
5:15, and there was a blue car in front of me. We
were both driving along Harbor Boulevard when a
white Ford suddenly shot out of a side street. It
drove right in front of the blue car. The driver tried
to stop, but it was impossible. He ran into the white
Ford.

1ST LAWYER: I see. Now, how fast was the car in front
of you going when the accident happened?
JOE: The blue car? 30 miles an hour. Certainly no more
than that.
1ST LAWYER: And the white Ford suddenly appeared
without any warning?
JOE: Yes, that's right.
1ST LAWYER: Thank you, Mr. Freeman.
2ND LAWYER: Mr. Freeman, how can you be sure the
blue car was only going 30?
JOE: Because I was only going 30, and the blue car
wasn't going any faster than I was.
2ND LAWYER: Are you sure of that? Absolutely
positive?
JOE: Yes, I am. I'm positive!
2ND LAWYER: Positive? How can you be so positive,
Mr. Freeman? Were you looking at your
speedometer when the accident happened?
JOE: Of course not. I was looking at the road ahead.
That's how I managed to see the accident!
2ND LAWYER: Well, if you weren't looking at your
speedometer, how can you possibly be sure how fast
you were going?
JOE: Because I never go faster than 30 on that road.
It's against the law, that's why!

Correct the statements
1. Joe was driving in front of the blue car.
2. The white Ford shot right in front of him.
3. The blue car was going about 50 miles an hour.
4. The blue car was going faster than Joe was.
5. Joe was looking at the speedometer when the
   accident happened.

Questions
1. Whose fault do you think the accident was? Say
   why.
2. Do you think the driver of the blue car was driving
   dangerously? Give reasons.
3. Ask and answer these questions about Joe when the
   accident happened:
   a. how fast?   c. from work or to work?
   b. looking at?
4. How does Joe know what speed he was going when
   the accident happened?
5. Who do you think the first lawyer is defending?
   Who do you think the second lawyer is defending?
   Give reasons.

e / Summary

Focal Points in this Unit

. Note the formation of the Past Continuous tense:
  a. I, he, she, it was / we, you, they were + verb-*ing*.
  Questions and negatives are formed like this:
  He wasn't / we weren't + verb-*ing*.
  Was he / were they + verb-*ing*?

. Remember that there is an important difference between two sentences like:
  He was crossing the street when he saw me.
  and:
  He stopped when he saw me.
  In these sentences, *he was crossing* is a background action; *he stopped* is a simple action.

f / Exercises for Homework

1. Do all the exercises and questions on pages 75 and 78.

2. **Invention Exercise**
  Example:
     CUES: to work this morning / an accident
  RESPONSE: **I was walking to work this morning when I saw an accident.**
        or: **John was riding to work this morning when he had an accident.**
  Cues:
  a. breakfast / the telephone
  b. television / doorbell
  c. my shirt / a button (off)
  d. along the sidewalk / a banana peel
  e. the guitar / a string
  f. newspaper / bus
  g. in the park / a friend
  h. tennis / rain
  i. homework / noise outside

3. Complete these sentences. (Use Simple Past or Continuous forms.)
  a. I was walking through the park yesterday when . . .
  b. When I opened the door, . . .
  c. It was snowing when . . .
  d. I was ringing the doorbell when . . .
  e. When I got to class, . . .

4. **Guided Composition**
  Read situations 1 and 2 on page 75 again very carefully. Then write about a short visit to a film studio. Begin like this:

  The other day I went to visit a film studio. When I got there, a friend met me, and we went straight to where they were shooting a scene for . . .

  Say what kind of film they were making, and describe what the different people were doing when you got there. Also describe what they all did when they stopped for the lunch break. Finally, describe what some of the people were doing when you left the studio later in the afternoon.

5. **Transfer Exercise**
  Write 5 sentences about yourself which are true.
  Use the tenses we have practiced in this unit.
  For example:
  I was driving to Boston last weekend when my car broke down.

  When my car broke down, I called a service station.
  Or:
  I got out of bed this morning when my alarm clock rang.

  When I got out of bed, the sun was shining in through the window.

14a
Will in Requests and Offers
and Future with **Will / Will have to / Will be able to**

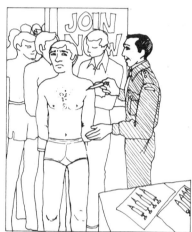

1

a. When / Fred / army?

b. What / doctor / going to do?

c. Fred ask?

d. doctor answer?

2

a. What / Susan ask Joe?

b. Where / Peter?

c. What / Peter / say?

3

a. What can't / woman?

b. What / have to do?

c. Where / to?

d. What / there?

4

a. What / Joe / a moment ago?

b. How / offer?

c. How / woman / thank him?

5

a. What / Joe doing?

b. What / Peter / say?

c. complicated?

6

a. How / Frank?

b. What / doctor / say?
(for a week)
(every six hours)

c. What / Frank / tomorrow?

"Will you . . . ?" in requests / *"I'll"* in offers of help
Will have to and **will be able to** as future expressions for __must__ and **can**
Reflexive Pronouns used emphatically as in "I can't do this myself"

14a

1

Fred Collins joined the army a few days ago. A doctor is going to give him an injection in the arm.

"Will it hurt?" Fred wants to know.

"No, don't worry. It won't hurt at all. You won't even feel it," the doctor is saying.
1. What is the doctor going to do?
2. What exactly is Fred's question?
3. What is the exact answer?
4. Ask questions with *Will.* Give short answers with *Yes, it / he will* or *No, it / he won't.*
   a. hurt
   b. Fred feel it
   c. be very pleasant

2

Susan finished writing a letter only a few minutes ago and she asked Joe to mail it. She said, "Will you mail this for me, Joe? It has to go out in today's mail."

Peter is going out for a walk. "I'll mail it for you. I'm going out for a walk anyway," he is saying.
1. What did Susan ask Joe to do a moment ago?
2. How exactly did she ask him to do this?
3. Why does Peter have his jacket on?
4. What is he saying?

3

The elderly woman cannot carry her suitcase herself. "I can't possibly carry this myself. I have to find a porter!" she is thinking. She is in San Francisco now. She is going to catch a bus to Sacramento. She will have to find a porter there too. She won't be able to carry the suitcase there either.
1. Where is the woman now?
2. What must she do now and why?
3. Where is she going?
4. What will she have to do there and why?

4

Joe is going to catch the same bus. He noticed the elderly woman a moment ago and offered to help her.

"I'll carry that suitcase for you. You can't possibly carry it yourself," he said. The woman is thanking him. "Thank you. That's very nice of you."
1. When did Joe notice her and what did he offer to do?
2. What exactly did he say?
3. What is the woman doing now?
4. What exactly is she saying?

5

Joe is looking at the engine of his car. There is something wrong with it and he does not think he can fix it himself. "I'll help you. Maybe we can do it ourselves!" Peter is saying. Actually it is something very complicated. Joe and Peter cannot possibly fix it themselves. They will have to get a mechanic.
1. What is Joe looking at and why?
2. Ask and answer the questions:
   a. Joe / fix it himself
   b. Peter think / themselves
3. What exactly is Peter saying?
4. What will they have to do and why?

6

Frank Martin is very sick. The doctor is talking to him.

"You'll have to stay in bed for a week and you'll have to take one of these pills every six hours."

Frank has a ticket for the big football game tomorrow. He won't be able to use it.
1. Why is the doctor there?
2. Ask questions about Frank with "Will he have to . . . ?" or "Will he be able to . . . ?" Answer "Yes, he will" or "No, he won't."
   a. in bed very long
   b. medicine very often
   c. the ticket
   d. the game tomorrow
   e. on television

14b FORMATION AND MANIPULATION

1 Use this table to ask someone else to do something for you. Imitate Susan's intonation in situation 2.

Will you	mail this letter carry this suitcase give Mr. Ellis this message play that record sing that song again	for	them? her? me? him? us?

2 With another person, carry on a conversation using this table. Imitate Joe's intonation in situation 4.

A:	I'll	carry that suitcase answer the phone do the dishes mail the letter close the window	for you.	B:	Thank you.	That's very	nice kind good helpful	of you.

3 How many sentences can you make from this table? Make at least twelve orally.

You	will / won't	have to be able to	work late see the boss go to that movie take the test mail the letter	tomorrow. some other time. later. next week.

Notice the question forms and the short answers:

Will you	be able to have to	come again?

Yes, I will / No, I won't.

Ask someone else questions with these cues:
(Tell that person to give short answers.)

see me this evening // play golf tomorrow //
work late this evening // give me an answer soon //
repair the car yourself // take it to a mechanic //

4   a. Look at these words and say them aloud:
     myself   himself   herself   itself   yourself   oursel*ves*   yoursel*ves*   themsel*ves*

  b. Now make sentences with those words and these
    cues:

Example: little girl / that heavy bag
That little girl cannot carry that heavy bag herself.
1. little girl / all that ice cream
2. We / all this work

3. Joe and Peter / all that work
4. Susan / all the dirty dishes
5. Bruce / all that food
6. I / this difficult question

  c. Notice that when we are speaking directly to more than one person, we use *yourselves*.
Example: All right, children. You'll have to clean up the room yourselves!

The Man Who Escaped
EPISODE 14

SUMMARY:(NOTE: *The summary now uses all tenses previously introduced.) In Chicago, Kincaid is very nervous because Fletcher is still free. Fletcher is driving to Chicago with Marilyn. He has asked her to help him find the real spies.*

Marilyn was an actress. She played small parts in movies and on television. Her life was full of surprises and she always seemed ready for anything. Perhaps this was why she did not
5 hesitate for even a second when Fletcher asked her to help him find the real spies.

"Will you tell me who we're looking for?" Marilyn asked.

Marilyn listened as Fletcher talked about
10 John Kincaid and the events that led up to the trial and imprisonment.

"And who is Hooper?" Marilyn asked.

"I wish I knew," Fletcher replied. "His name came up several times when Kincaid and
15 I were trying to find out who was giving away secret information."

"So why do you suspect Kincaid? If he was really involved . . ."

Fletcher interrupted, "You're forgetting one
20 important thing. Kincaid lied at the trial. He denied that we were working on the case together. He told the court he suspected me all the time."

Marilyn slowed down the car. "We're
25 getting near Chicago," she said. "Are we going to have any trouble finding Kincaid?"

"I don't think so," Fletcher replied. "There's a place called the Ringside Club, and I understand Kincaid spends lots of time there.
30 We'll have to go there."

Rossi was on the phone with his chief, Howard Becker, in Washington. He was writing down Kincaid's name. "What's so interesting about Kincaid?" Rossi was asking.
35 "Why do you want me to go to Chicago to look for him?"

"We've just learned a few things about Kincaid," Howard Becker answered. "Fletcher might be innocent after all. But it's
40 only a possibility. We want to see what Kincaid does if Fletcher contacts him."

Rossi was even more surprised now. "I don't understand. What do you think Kincaid might do?" he asked.

45 "Kincaid might try to kill Fletcher if he's really afraid of him."

"But isn't that dangerous? I mean, if Fletcher's innocent, Kincaid might kill him . . . and if he isn't innocent, we're letting him go
50 free. After all, Fletcher might kill Kincaid . . . or someone else!"

"That's a chance we'll have to take, Rossi!" Becker said seriously.

14d FURTHER PRACTICE

1 / Practice Situations

Make 2 sentences for each situation, one with
"He'll / she'll / they'll have to . . ." and one with
"He / she / they won't be able to . . ."

EXAMPLE SITUATION:
Jane usually catches the 8:15 bus. The next one is at
8:40. It is 8:20 now, and she is running out of the
house.

EXAMPLE SENTENCES:
1. **She won't be able to catch the 8:15 bus.**
2. **She'll have to catch the 8:40.**

Situations:
a. Bob has just broken his leg. He wanted to play
   basketball this year.
b. Joe likes to put cream in his coffee, but they only
   have milk in the refrigerator.
c. Frank wanted to leave work early today. He
   wanted to see a football game. The foreman asked
   all the men to work overtime.
d. Laura and Bruce wanted to drive to Las Vegas, but
   the car broke down yesterday. Laura has just
   reserved two seats on Omega Airlines instead.

2 / Conversation

   Mr. Ellis, Jane's boss, is talking to Jane on the office
intercom.
MR. ELLIS: Do you think you could possibly work late
   this evening, Jane? I'm afraid there's some work we
   really have to finish and I can't do it all myself.
JANE: Work late? I . . . I suppose so, if it's necessary.
MR. ELLIS: Thank you. You'll only have to work about
   an hour overtime. That's all. (hangs up)
JANE: (to herself, while dialing) Now I'll have to call
   Jim and tell him. He won't like it.
JIM: Hello?
JANE: Is that you, Jim? This is Jane. Uh . . . I'm afraid
   I won't be able to meet you at 6:30. It'll have to be
   later than that.
JIM: What? You mean you're going to be late again?
JANE: Now listen, Jim, please. It isn't my fault. I have

to work late this evening and then after work I'll
have to go home. I can't possibly go to the
restaurant straight from work!
JIM: It's always something, isn't it? When will you be
   able to meet me, then?
JANE: Don't worry. I'll be there at 7:30.
JIM: At 7:30? But we're going to a movie after dinner.
   Remember?
JANE: I know . . . and it starts at 7:45. We'll just have
   to miss it this evening, that's all. We'll be able to see
   it some other time.
JIM: Oh, no we won't! Tonight's the last night!
JANE: Oh, dear . . . I suppose I'll just have to come
   straight from work then.
JIM: Yes, you will. Meet me at the restaurant at 7:00!
JANE: All right. I'll be there. See you then!

Questions
1. What does Mr. Ellis ask Jane to do?
2. How exactly does he ask her to work late?
3. Where is Jane going to meet Jim?
4. What does she want to do before she meets him?
5. What are her exact words when she tells Jim this?
6. What does she say when Jim tells her about the
   movie at 7:45?
7. Ask if they will be able to see the movie tomorrow
   (and answer).
8. What does Jane finally decide she'll have to do?

e / Summary

Focal Points in this Unit

1. Remember how we use *will* when asking someone to do something:
    Will you mail this for me?
    Will you carry this for me?
   and how we use *I'll* when we offer to help someone do something:
    I'll mail it for you.
    I'll carry that suitcase for you.

2. Remember what we say when someone offers to help:
    Thank you. That's very kind of you.
                      nice
                      good
                      helpful

3. Remember the way we express *can* and *must* in future time.
    I will have to see him tomorrow.
    I will be able to work late tomorrow.
    I won't have to take the test.
    I won't be able to come tonight.
   The short answers to questions like *Will you be able to . . . ?* and *Will you have to . . . ?* are *Yes, I will* and *No, I won't.*

4. Remember the reflexive (emphatic) pronouns *myself, yourself, himself, herself, itself, ourselves, yourselves, themselves:*
    Maybe we can do it ourselves.

f / Exercises for Homework

1. Do all the exercises on pages 81, 82 and 84.

2. **Invention Exercise**
   Write 2 sentences for each of the cues, one sentence with "I'll . . ." and one with "Will you . . . ?"
   Example: that bag
   I'll carry that bag for you.
   Will you carry that bag for me?

    a. that letter
    b. the tickets for the concert
    c. a porter
    d. old car
    e. one of those pills
    f. the dog
    g. some coffee
    h. a newspaper
    i. to the movies
    j. the telephone

3. **Guided Composition**
   Write two short personal notes (of 4 or 5 lines each):
   a. to a friend, saying that you are sorry you won't be able to go to San Francisco with him or her as arranged (and give a reason).
   b. to your boss (or teacher) explaining why you won't be able to attend a certain meeting or class (and give a reason).
   Before you write the notes, read situations 3, 5 and 6 (on page 81) and the Conversation (on page 84) again, and notice how we use the following phrases which you will need:
    I am afraid . . . // I can't possibly . . . // I'll have to . . . // my fault // I'll just have to . . . // some other time // I won't be able to . . . either // I suppose . . . //

4. **Transfer Exercise**
   Write true sentences about yourself, relatives or friends using *will / won't have to* and *will / won't be able to.*
   Examples:
   I won't be able to play tennis tomorrow.

   My father will have to sell his car soon; it's already fifteen years old.

traigiuóu, tuóng phan.

1

a. What / police / ticket agent?
b. flight / yet?

2

a. Who / Peter / with?
b. How long / bathroom?
c. What / Joe / want?

3

a. sun shining / started?
b. rain / now?

4

a. What / Bruce's secretary / ask?
b. Where / Mr. Foster?
c. catch him?

5

a. Where / Jane?
b. What / noticed?
c. What / just said?
d. boyfriend's question?
e. Jane's answer?

6

a. Which movie / Peter?
b. Who / noticed?
c. Where / boyfriend?
d. Peter's question?
e. Jane's answer?

1

The police are asking the ticket agent about a man they think might be on the flight to Chicago.

"Have you seen this man?"

"No, I haven't. At least, I don't think so."

"Has the Chicago flight left yet?"

"No, it hasn't."

1. Why are the police asking the ticket agent about the man in the photograph?
2. Ask and answer the questions:
   a. Chicago flight / yet
   b. ticket agent / the man
3. Is the ticket agent sure?
4. What exactly does he say?

2

Peter is staying with Joe and Susan. He has been in the bathroom for half an hour. Joe wants to get in and has just asked, "Have you finished yet?"

"Yes, I have. I'll be out in a second," Peter is telling him. He has taken a shower and has just shaved.

1. Who is Peter staying with?
2. Where is he now? Ask "How long . . . ?"
3. What has Joe just asked?
4. Ask and answer questions about Peter:
   a. finished yet
   b. a bath or a shower
   c shaved

3

It was raining when Bruce started the conference. He has just noticed that it has stopped and that the sun has come out.

"Look! The rain's stopped. It might clear up this evening."

"I hope so," the other man is saying.

1. What was the weather like when the conference started?
2. What two things have just happened?
3. What has Bruce just said?
4. Is he sure it is going to clear up?
5. What is the other man's answer?

4

Bruce's secretary has just stopped another secretary in the outer office.

"Have you seen Mr. Foster?" she wants to know.

"Yes, I have. I saw him only a moment ago. He's just gone down that hallway." She might catch him if she hurries.

1. What has Bruce's secretary just done?
2. What does she want to know?
3. Has the other secretary seen him?
4. Ask when (and answer).
5. What has Bruce just done?

5

Jane has just come out of the movie theater. She has just noticed that she doesn't have her umbrella.

"I've left it inside!" she has just said.

"Are you sure you had it when we went in?" her boyfriend is asking.

"Yes, I am. At least, I think so."

1. What have Jane and her boyfriend just done?
2. Why has Jane suddenly stopped?
3. What does she think she has done with her umbrella?
4. What is her boyfriend's question?
5. What is her answer?

6

Peter has seen the same movie too. He has just noticed Jane. Her boyfriend has gone back into the theater. Peter is sure he has seen her before. "Excuse me," he has just said, "haven't we met somewhere before?"

"No, I don't think so," Jane is saying to him.

1. Why is Peter in front of the theater?
2. Why has he stopped?
3. What has he just said and why?
4. What is Jane's answer?

15b FORMATION AND MANIPULATION

1 Pronunciation
Notice that the full forms of *have* and *has* are used in questions but that in normal conversation the contracted forms *'s* and *'ve* are used in statements. Practice these forms in class and notice the teacher's pronunciation and intonation.

Examples:
a. We've (/ 'v /) just arrived.
b. Have (/ həv /) you eaten?

c. He's (/ 'z /) just arrived.
d. Has (/ həz /) he arrived?

2

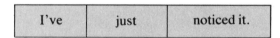

A	B	C
I've	just	noticed it.

a. You know what kind of words can go into box A, so look at the situations on page 87 to find words to go in box C.
b. Make six sentences from the words you have found.
c. Now make questions using the same words you used for exercise **b**.
   Example: **Have you just noticed it?**

3

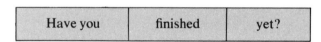

A	B	C
Have you	finished	yet?

a. Find words to replace those in boxes A and B. You can find them in the situations on page 87.
b. Now, ask two questions about each situation on page 87.
   Example: **Have the police found the man yet?** (situation 1)

4 Use *might* for future possibilities (see situations 3 and 4).
Make sentences from these cues:
a. rain soon / come tomorrow / buy a new one / see the movie / ask her / get one / lose it / sell them
b. Now think of some things you might do in the future, and make up five or six sentences.

5 Notice how we use the words THINK and HOPE to say "yes."
Question: Will the weather be good tomorrow?   Answer: I think *so*. (I hope *so*.)

Note especially how we say "no" with these words.
Question: Will it rain tomorrow?   Answer: I *don't* think so. (I hope *not*.)

The Man Who Escaped

EPISODE 15

SUMMARY: *While they were driving to Chicago, Fletcher told Marilyn that John Kincaid lied at the trial and that the real spies were Kincaid and a man named Hooper. Rossi's chief, Howard Becker, has told Rossi to go to Chicago to find Kincaid.*

In a hotel room in Chicago, Fletcher walked back and forth nervously. Marilyn had gone out shopping. He tried to sleep, but he couldn't. He had a lot on his mind. It was after
5 dark when Marilyn came back. She was carrying two large shopping bags.

"Where have you been? You've been gone for hours!" he said.

"Yes, I've been busy. Here. Try these
10 things on," she answered. She opened the bags quickly and gave him a suit, shoes and a shirt and tie. There was also an expensive-looking coat with a fur collar. Fletcher put on the clothes unwillingly. "I'll have to change my
15 appearance more than this!" he said.

"Of course you will," she answered. "And I've got just the things you'll need."

First Marilyn dyed Fletcher's hair gray. Then she used some stage makeup to give him
20 a much older face. She led him to a full-length mirror. Fletcher was surprised when he saw himself. An old man stared back at him in the mirror. His gray hair and expensive coat gave him a distinguished look.
25 "And now," said Marilyn, "you'll have to do more than just look like an old man. You'll have to walk, talk and act like one too!" And she taught him exactly what to do.

"You learn fast. We can go to the Ringside
30 Club now," she said finally.

"What do you mean 'we'? You can't come with me. It might be dangerous," he said. Marilyn was already putting on her coat. Her answer was simple, "If you want my help,

35 you'll have to take me with you. Besides, things are just beginning to get interesting! Let's go."

Rossi spent the day in Chicago collecting information about John Kincaid. He got an old
40 picture of him from the newspaper files, his license number and type of car and finally his home and work addresses. He also learned that John Kincaid often went to the Ringside Club. Rossi looked for Kincaid at his store and at
45 home but he didn't find him. It was 9 o'clock. He decided to go to the Ringside Club and see if Kincaid was there.

15d FURTHER PRACTICE

1 / Conversation for Paired Practice

Read this conversation, and use the cues to make others like it.

MODEL: A: **I've just been to the new Chinese restaurant.**
　　　　B: **Oh! Have you? I've just been to an Indian restaurant.**

Cues:

a.　A: a new Japanese car
　　B: a German car

b.　A: a book by Frederick Nolan
　　B: a book by James Michener

c.　A: a new job in Beverly Hills
　　B: a new job in Hollywood

d.　A: lunch in the new cafeteria
　　B: lunch in the coffee shop around the corner

e.　A: the new movie at the Times
　　B: the new movie at the Plaza

f.　A: a new stereo
　　B: a new color TV

2 / Conversation

Laura has a car of her own now. There is something wrong with it. She has just driven into the service department of the new car dealer's.

MECHANIC: Good morning, Mrs. Foster. What can we do for you?

LAURA: I'm afraid there's something wrong with my car. I've just noticed that it's been using a lot of gas lately, far more than usual.

MECHANIC: Oh? Well, we'd better have a look at it, then. Can you leave it with us now?

LAURA: I suppose I'll have to. Do you think it might be something serious?

MECHANIC: I wouldn't think so, but you never know, of course. It might be a major problem.

LAURA: I certainly hope not. I want to use it this evening. Do you think I'll be able to? I mean, will it be ready by then?

MECHANIC: It might be. It all depends on what the trouble is. Do you think you could give us a call around 5 o'clock? We'll know by then.

LAURA: Around 5:00? All right.

AT FIVE O'CLOCK THAT EVENING

CASHIER: Hello. Broadway Motors.

LAURA: Hello. This is Mrs. Foster. I'm calling about my car.

CASHIER: Oh, hello, Mrs. Foster. They have just finished your car. It's ready now.

LAURA: Oh, good! What was the trouble?

CASHIER: Let's see . . . it wasn't anything very serious. There was a leak in the gas tank. That was covered under the warranty. Anyway, they've taken care of it now and you can pick up your car any time.

LAURA: Good. What time do you close?

CASHIER: At 6:00.

LAURA: Oh, fine. I can get there by then. Good-bye.

CASHIER: Bye.

Questions

(When Laura takes the car to the service department in the morning)

1.　Correct the statements:
　　a.　Laura noticed the trouble several days ago.
　　b.　The mechanic says the car will definitely be ready in the evening.
　　c.　He thinks it is something serious.

2.　Answer the questions:
　　a.　Why does she hope it isn't anything serious?
　　b.　What are the two things the mechanic asks her to do?

(When Laura calls at 5 o'clock)

1.　Correct the statements:
　　a.　The men have not finished the car yet.
　　b.　The garage closes at 7:00.

2.　Answer the questions:
　　a.　What exactly was the trouble?
　　b.　What have the men done about it?

e / Summary

Focal Points in this Unit

1. Remember how we use the word *just* with
has/have done and *did*. Notice the position of the
word *just:*
>He has *just* gone down that hallway.
>He *just* went down that hallway.

Remember that we use *just* with *has / have done*
and *did* when we are talking about something that
happened a few seconds ago.

2. Remember that we also use *has / have done* when
we are talking about something in the past, but give
no indication of the time:
Example:
>Have you (ever) seen this man (before)?

3. Notice the form of the verb after *might:*
>It might *clear up* this evening.

Remember that *might* is the same for all persons,
and that we can use it in the present and in the
future. In a sentence like "They think he *might be*
on the train," *might be* means "is possibly;" in a
sentence like "She *might catch* him if she hurries,"
might catch means "maybe will catch."

4. Remember these phrases with *think* and *hope.*
Notice the different way we form the negatives:
>I think so.   I hope so.
>I don't think so.   I hope not.

f / Exercises for Homework

1. Do all the exercises on pages 87, 88 and 90.

2. Change the form of these verbs and put them into
the appropriate sentence:
>see, leave, come, go, meet, notice, stop, take,
>tell, be

a. Haven't I . . . that girl somewhere before?
b. Have you . . . care of that noise in the engine
yet?
c. He's . . . in the bathroom a long time!

d. Good! It's . . . raining. We can go out in the yard
again.
e. Has he . . . you his favorite story?
f. Oh, dear! It's going to rain and I've . . . my
umbrella at home.
g. "Where's Bill?" "Oh, he's . . . to the movies."
h. Have you . . . the new film about King Kong?
i. I've just . . . from a very important meeting.
j. I've just . . . that Mary has cut her hair.

3. **Guided Composition**
Read the first half of the Conversation between
Laura and the mechanic on page 90 again, and then
write a conversation between a woman and a
salesperson in a watch repair shop. There is
something wrong with the woman's watch and she
has just taken it in for repair. Use as many of the
phrases and sentence patterns as you can, and
begin like this:

WOMAN: Good morning.
SALESPERSON: Good morning. What can I do for
you?
WOMAN: Well, I'm afraid . . .

4. **Transfer Exercise**
Write 5 sentences about things which have just
happened.
Examples:
We have just finished Exercise 3.

**I have just spoken to my girl / boyfriend on the
phone.**

My parents have just left for Miami.

1

a. What / typist just?

b. What / Jane / ask?

c. typist's questions?

d. the answers?

2

a. Who / Peter / talk to?

b. Peter's questions?

c. the girl's answers?

3

a. What / George Upwell?

b. Who / talk to?

c. ever / jewels? factory? soldier? cowboy? prison? teacher?

4

a. When / jewels? prison? etc.

b. George Upwell's answers?

5

a. Laura ever / Rome? etc.

b. When / Rome? etc.

c. Laura's answers?

16a

1

Jane is working in the office. One of the typists has just come to work. She is late again. She is asking Jane about her boss. He often comes in late too.

"Has my boss come yet?"

"Yes, he has. He's in his office now."

"When did he get here?"

"He came very early. He noticed you weren't here."

1. What is Jane doing?
2. What has one of the typists just done?
3. Ask these questions about her boss:
   a. yet   c. What / notice
   b. early or late

2

Peter Freeman is talking to one of his girlfriends.

"Have you seen that movie yet?"

"Yes, I have. I saw it last week."

"What did you think of it?"

"I didn't like it very much."

Ask these questions about Peter's girlfriend:

a. the movie yet   c. like it
b. When

3

George Upwell is a famous writer. He has done a lot of things in his life. He is talking to a television interviewer now. "I've smuggled jewels, sold used cars and worked in a factory. I've been a soldier, a waiter and a cowboy. I've also been a teacher and I've even been in prison!"

1. What is George Upwell?
2. Ask these questions about him:
   a. many things   c. many jobs
   b. many places
3. Ask questions with "Has he ever . . .?"
   a. jewels   d. soldier   g. teacher
   b. used cars   e. waiter   h. in prison
   c. factory   f. cowboy

4

The interviewer is asking him when he did all these things. "When did you smuggle jewels? When were you in prison?" "I smuggled jewels in 1960. I was in prison in 1961." The interviewer is going to ask him some more questions.

1. What are the interviewer's first two questions?
2. What are Upwell's first two answers?
3. Ask some more questions about his life with "When . . .?" and answer them.

5

One of Laura's friends is asking her about all the vacation trips she has taken and all the places she has been to.

"Have you ever been to Rome?"

"Yes, I have. I was there in 1974."

"Have you ever been to Mexico City, Tokyo or Rio?"

"Yes, I've been to all those places."

"Oh? When were you in Mexico City . . . and when were you in Tokyo and Rio?"

1. What is Laura's friend asking her about?
2. Ask questions about Laura first with "Has she ever . . .?" and then with "When . . .?" (and answer the questions).

16b FORMATION AND MANIPULATION

1 Pronunciation
  a. In short answers, *have, has, is, was* are stressed and, therefore, you pronounce the full form of each one.
   Examples: Yes, I háve.   Yes, he ís.
         Yes, he hás.   Yes, she wás.
  b. In questions starting *Have you . . .?* or *Has she . . .?*, some other word is usually stressed in the sentence and, therefore, a reduced (shortened) form of *have, has, is, was* is used.
   Examples: Have you ever driven a cár?   Is he a famous wríter?
         Has he ever beén here before?   Was she in Róme last year?
  c. In *When was that?* the stress is on *thát* and, therefore, a reduced (shortened) form of *was* is used.
   Example: When was (/ w'z /) that?

2 Look at these verbs: (They come from Units 12-16.)

	1	2			1	2
see	saw	seen		come	came	come
leave	left	left		stop	stopped	stopped
go	went	gone		run	ran	run
meet	met	met		write	wrote	written

  a. Read the following conversation. Observe where verb forms like *saw* (1) and *seen* (2) are.
   A: Have you ever seen that movie?
   B: Yes, I have.
   A: When did you see it?
   B: I saw it last week.
  b. You can use other time expressions to answer the question *When did you see it?*
   Examples: in 1968 / last year / yesterday / two weeks ago / a minute ago / a couple of days ago
  c. Use the verbs in columns 1 and 2 and the time expressions in exercise **b** to make a short dialog like the one in exercise **a**. Look at the situations on page 93 to make additional dialogs.
  d. Now, practice using *When was that?* in place of *When did you see it?* and make dialogs as in exercise **c**.

The Man Who Escaped

EPISODE 16

SUMMARY: *In Chicago, Marilyn helped Fletcher disguise himself as an old man. Then they went to the Ringside Club to look for Kincaid. Rossi has also gone to Chicago. He has decided to go to the Ringside Club to look for Kincaid too.*

Marilyn and Fletcher walked into the Ringside Club and sat down at a table in the lounge. Several people looked at them curiously as they entered. The club was crowded and noisy.
5 A band was playing.

"I didn't think it would be like this," Marilyn said. Fletcher was not listening to her. His eyes were searching all around the room for the one face that he would recognize instantly.
10 "It's nearly nine o'clock and Kincaid isn't here!" he said after a few minutes.

"Surely you didn't expect to walk in and find him, just like that!"

"No, I guess not."

15 When the band stopped playing and the club was quiet for a few minutes, Fletcher called the headwaiter.

"Yes," the headwaiter said as he walked over to the table, "What can I get you?"
20 In his weak old man's voice, Fletcher answered, "Nothing, actually. I just wanted to ask you a question."

"Certainly, sir," the headwaiter said.

"Does a man named . . . John Kincaid . . .
25 ever come in here?" Fletcher asked.

Neither Fletcher nor Marilyn noticed the reaction on the face of the man sitting at the next table when Fletcher said Kincaid's name.

"Do you mean *Colonel* Kincaid . . . the
30 owner of the antique store on Jackson Boulevard?"

"Yes, yes . . . !" Fletcher answered slowly. "That's the one . . . *Colonel* John Kincaid, the one with the antique shop. Has he been in here
35 this evening?"

"No, I don't think so," the headwaiter said.

"Wasn't that a little dangerous?" Marilyn asked when the headwaiter left.

"I guess it was," Fletcher answered. "But
40 I've got to work fast. I've got to find Kincaid before the police find me!"

Marilyn and Fletcher walked to a taxi parked in front of the Ringside Club. They did not notice the man that followed them out of the
45 club. He got in the taxi just behind theirs.

"Where to . . . ?" the driver asked.

"Jackson Boulevard. Where the antique stores are," Marilyn told the driver.

After a few minutes, the driver turned onto
50 Jackson Boulevard and slowed down. "Well, here we are. There are quite a few antique stores around here. Where do you want to stop?"

"Let us off at the corner," Marilyn said.
55 Marilyn and Fletcher walked along the street slowly, looking into each store. Suddenly, Fletcher saw something in a store window. There was a sign that said "Antique Military Weapons," and there was a large display of old
60 pistols.

"Of course!" Fletcher exclaimed. "Colonel Kincaid . . . ! This must be the place!"

16d FURTHER PRACTICE

1 / Invention Exercise

1. Make questions from the cues with this model:

  MODEL: Have you ever . . . ?
  CUE: spaghetti
  RESPONSE: **Have you ever eaten spaghetti?**
  or: **Have you ever cooked spaghetti?**

Cues:
a. Guam
b. modern furniture
c. that book
d. a jet
e. a Japanese movie
f. the President
g. that girl to the movies
h. a Rolls-Royce
i. Switzerland
j. any stories by Ernest Hemingway

2. Now use the questions you have made to begin conversations. Use this model:

  MODEL: A: **Have you ever been to Guam?**
  B: **Yes, I have.**
  A: **When were you there?**
  B: **I went there last year.**

2 / Conversation

Jane is in the watch department of a large store.
JANE: Excuse me. Do you repair watches?
SALESMAN: Yes, we do.
JANE: Oh, good. Would you look at mine? It's stopped.
SALESMAN: Certainly. Hmm . . . when did it stop?
JANE: Only yesterday. Can you do anything about it?
SALESMAN: I think so. Just leave it with me.
JANE: Oh, good. When will it be ready?
SALESMAN: This time next week. Now, you'll need a receipt.
JANE: Oh, yes. I mustn't forget that.
SALESMAN: No. You wouldn't be able to claim your watch without it.
JANE: All right. Well, thank you. Good-bye.

SALESMAN: Good-bye . . . Wait a minute, Miss! You've dropped something. Excuse me! Miss! You've dropped something!

ONE WEEK LATER

SALESGIRL: May I help you?
JANE: I hope so. I brought my watch in to be fixed, but now I've lost the receipt.
SALESGIRL: Lost the receipt? Oh, that's too bad.
JANE: Can't I just describe the watch to you?
SALESGIRL: I'm afraid not. Only the manager can help you and he's gone to lunch. He left only five minutes ago.
JANE: Oh, no! I think it was the manager who waited on me.
SALESGIRL: Just a minute. When did you bring the watch in?
JANE: A week ago at this time, during my lunch hour.
SALESGIRL: And was your watch a small gold *Automex?*
JANE: Yes, that's right. How did you know?
SALESGIRL: Because your receipt is still here. You dropped it when you left. The manager tried to catch you, but he couldn't.

Questions
1. What does Jane say about her watch when she brings it in?
2. What is the manager's exact question when she says this?
3. According to the manager, why does Jane need a receipt?
4. What exactly does he shout when she leaves?
5. Why is the receipt still there when Jane comes back?

Recall
Without looking at the conversation, try to remember the part between the salesgirl and Jane ("One Week Later").
SALESGIRL: help?
JANE: hope // watch / to be repaired // the receipt //
SALESGIRL: bad // only the manager // just / lunch / 5 minutes ago //

e / Summary

Focal Points in this Unit

1. In this unit, we have practiced and contrasted two tenses, the Present Perfect *has / have done* and the Simple Past *did.*
   a. Just look again at the types of sentences we have practiced with *has / have done:*
      1. She has just come to work.
      2. Has the boss come yet?
      3. He has done a lot of things in his life.
      4. Have you ever been to Rome?
      (There is no mention of a specific time.)
   b. And look at the types of sentence we have practiced with *did:*
      1. When did he come?
      2. I saw it last week.
      3. What did you think of it (the movie)?
      (The speaker knows when the other person saw the movie; there is a definite time element.)

2. Look at these two sentences:
   a. He's *gone* to lunch.
   b. I've *been* out to lunch.
   Sentence **a** tells us that he is not here now; he is probably eating now.
   Sentence **b** tells us that the person has gone to and come back from lunch.

3. Remember that the question *What did you think of it?* means "What was your opinion of it?"

f / Exercises for Homework

1. Do all the exercises on pages 93 and 96.

2. Supply the correct form of the verb (*have done* or *did*) in parentheses.
   a. I . . . my old car last week. (sell)
   b. . . . you . . . anything from your brother yet? (hear)
   c. We . . . John's new car. (just see)
   d. So you're back at last! Where . . . you . . .? (be)
   e. They . . . a lot of cake last night at the party. (eat)
   f. Excuse me! I think you . . . this purse a moment ago. (drop)
   g. He . . . out of the meeting a moment ago. You can speak to him now. (come)
   h. He's still in prison because he . . . some jewels last year. (smuggle)
   i. . . . it . . . raining yet? (stop)
   j. Who . . . you the last time, sir? (wait on)

3. **Guided Composition**
   You are a radio news reporter and you have just been sent to Forest Park where there is some trouble. Write down what you say as you comment on the scene, paying attention to the use of *is / doing, has / have done, has / have been doing* and *did.*
   Begin like this:
   > I arrived here in Forest Park about 10 minutes ago. There is a large crowd of about 200 people here . . .

   Finish the short report by describing how the police came, and how all the people left without violence, using these cues:
   > an hour or more // most / standing / some / sitting / grass // at the moment / very peaceful // young man / just finish / speech // start / half an hour ago //

4. **Transfer Exercise**
   Write a number of sentences about yourself using these examples:
   I've never been to China, but I've been to Japan. That was 3 years ago.

   I've never worked in a store, but I've worked in a factory. That was last year.
   (or: **I've never worked in a store, but I've worked in a factory. In fact, I work in a factory now.**)

1

a. When / phone?
b. Who / person / speak to?
c. When / Bruce / back?
d. secretary / saying?

2

a. Why / Joe / the dishes?
b. Where / Susan?
c. Joe / like / dishes?
d. Joe / saying to Peter?

3

a. When / Fred / army?
b. Fred / like / soldier?
c. Where / Fred / now?
d. Fred saying to the sergeant?

4

a. Where / Frank?
b. What / he / give up?
c. Who / talk to?
d. Frank / saying to Susan?

5

a. chairman shouting now?
b. a few minutes ago?

1

The phone rang a few seconds ago. Someone wants to speak to Bruce.

"I'm awfully sorry," his secretary is saying. "Mr. Foster has gone out. He'll be back at 3 o'clock. Would you mind calling him then?"

1. Ask and answer the questions:
   a. When / the phone   c. When / back
   b. Bruce there
2. The person on the phone can speak to Bruce at 3:00; what does Bruce's secretary say to the person?

2

Joe Freeman has to do the dishes because Susan's father is in the hospital and she has gone to visit him. Joe does not like washing dishes. In fact, he hates washing them.

"I wonder if you'd mind helping me?" he is saying to Peter.

1. Ask and answer the questions:
   a. Why / Joe the dishes
   b. like . . . ?
2. What is it that he hates doing?
3. What is he saying to Peter?

3

Fred Collins joined the army a few months ago, but he does not like being a soldier. In fact, he hates it. He hates carrying a heavy rifle and wearing a uniform. He also hates getting up early. All the other soldiers have already gotten up. "I wonder if you'd mind closing that window, Sergeant?" Fred is saying.

1. Ask and answer the questions:
   a. When / the army   b. like / a soldier
2. Ask if he hates doing these things:
   a. a heavy rifle   c. up early
   b. a uniform
3. What is he saying to the sergeant?
4. Why do you think the sergeant is angry?

4

Frank Martin is in the hospital. He has had to give up eating fried foods, desserts and anything sweet. The doctor says these things are very bad for him. Susan is visiting him now. "Susan, I wonder if you'd mind bringing me a box of chocolates the next time you come?" he is saying to her.

1. What are the things Frank cannot have?
2. What is he saying to Susan now?
3. Do you think she will?

5

This is a public meeting. It has gotten out of control. The chairman is telling people to stop doing various things. At first he tried to be polite. "Would you mind not waving that sign around?" he said a few minutes ago. Now he is shouting, "Stop waving that sign!" A group of people are shouting, "We want Johnson!" Another group is singing, and two men are arguing loudly. A few men are leaving the meeting.

1. What sort of meeting is this and what has happened?
2. What did the chairman say to the man with the sign a few minutes ago?
3. What is he shouting now?
4. He tried to be polite with the other people too. What do you think he said to them?

17b FORMATION AND MANIPULATION

1 Intonation

   a. Notice the secretary's intonation, situation 1, page 99: *Would you mind calling him then?* Practice saying this just as she does. Then use the same intonation pattern in the following sentences:

      1. Would you mind sitting there?   4. Would you mind having tea?

      2. Would you mind coming in?   5. Would you mind asking him?

      3. Would you mind going out?

   b. Notice the very polite form *I wonder if you'd mind . . . -ing?* Practice the intonation of this form as Joe uses it in situation 2, page 99. Use the three examples in situations 2, 3 and 4 on page 99 to practice this pattern.

2 Make questions (with and without *not*):

Would you Would they Would she Would he	mind	(not)	waiting for me? coming back later? using an old one? seeing him tomorrow?

3 With someone else, practice asking and answering the questions using the following very frequent short answer forms:

   a. Yes, I (etc.) would.   e. Of course he (etc.) would (n't).

   b. No, I (etc.) wouldn't.   f. I expect so.

   c. Not at all.   g. I don't think so.

   d. Of course not.

4 With someone else, use the table below and ask questions. Use the answers given in **3**.

I wonder	if	you'd they'd she'd he'd	mind	helping me? opening the door? asking her? coming in?

5 Using these verbs—*stop, give up, hate, like*—make sentences about these things: baseball, dancing, TV, candy, hospitals, gardens, flowers, movies, work, swimming, football, ping-pong.

The Man Who Escaped
EPISODE 17

SUMMARY: *Fletcher, disguised as an old man, went to the Ringside Club with Marilyn. Kincaid was not there. The headwaiter told them Colonel Kincaid owned an antique store. Fletcher and Marilyn didn't notice that the man sitting at the next table was listening to them. The man followed them when they left the club. They went to Jackson Boulevard and found Kincaid's antique store.*

At the Ringside Club, Rossi sat down and pretended to listen to the music. Actually, he was studying the faces of the people in the club. If John Kincaid was there, he would
5 recognize him at once.

"Is everything all right, sir?" the headwaiter asked as he approached the table.

Rossi nodded and then asked, "Is it always
10 this crowded?"

The headwaiter laughed, "You should see this place on a Saturday night!"

"I'm looking for a friend of mine," Rossi told the headwaiter. "His name is John Kincaid. Do you know him, by any chance?"
15 The headwaiter hesitated for a minute. "John Kincaid . . . ? Uh, . . . no, I don't believe I do . . . !"

"This is Antonio at the club," the headwaiter said in a low voice.
20 "Yes, Antonio. What's the problem . . . ?" the voice at the other end of the phone said.

"There's no problem, Colonel, but I thought you might like to know . . . Some people have been asking about you tonight."
25 "People . . . ? What people? Who are they . . . ?"

"I don't know, Colonel. I've never seen them before. First, there was an old man with a woman. Then a few minutes ago, another man
30 came in and asked if I knew you."

There was a long silence. Then the voice said, "Tell me about the man . . . what did he look like?"

Kincaid stared at the phone as it rang. He
35 was sure Fletcher had managed to get his phone number from Antonio. Finally, he picked up the receiver.

"Hello . . . "

"Kincaid . . . ?"

"Hooper . . . !" said Kincaid, taking a deep
40 breath. "Where are you?"

"Never mind that now. I've got something to tell you. A young woman and an old man are looking for you. They were at the club asking
45 questions. I followed them and they went straight to your store. I don't know who they are, but be careful!"

"Hooper, I think Fletcher's in Chicago! Antonio . . . !" Kincaid began. Hooper inter-
50 rupted him, "I'll talk to you when I see you tomorrow night. Be there at 11 o'clock!"

Kincaid did not sleep well that night.

17d FURTHER PRACTICE

1 / Invention Exercise

1. Make questions with *stop* using the cues:
   - MODEL: Would you please *stop . . . -ing . . .*?
   - CUE: that terrible noise
   - RESPONSE: **Would you please stop making that terrible noise?**

   Cues:
   a. those letters
   b. that guitar
   c. the radio
   d. those awful records
   e. the phone so much
   f. your dictionary
   g. so much candy
   h. that book
   i. that song

2. Now use the same cues for examples with the verb *mind*:
   - CUE: that terrible noise
   - RESPONSE: **Would you mind not making that terrible noise?**
   - CUE: those letters
   - RESPONSE: **Would you mind typing those letters now, please?**

2 / Conversation

Mr. Kerr is sitting in his living room. He can't concentrate on his reading because he's worried about Bob, his 16-year-old son.

MR. KERR: (hears noise) Bob? Is that you?

BOB: (from kitchen) Yes, Dad. I'm home.

MR. KERR: (puzzled) Is everything all right?

BOB: (comes in) Uh . . . what do you mean?

MR. KERR: Well, it's only 9 o'clock. I didn't think you'd be back this early.

BOB: I didn't want you to start worrying. I knew you'd be pretty nervous, so . . .

MR. KERR: What gave you that idea?

BOB: When you ride with me, you're always a nervous wreck.

MR. KERR: I wish you'd stop saying that, son. I feel perfectly safe when you're driving. Oh, maybe sometimes you drive a little too close to the car in front of you . . .

BOB: I want to talk to you about that.

MR. KERR: What?

BOB: Driving too close—tailgating. I know you hate it. I've decided not to do it anymore.

MR. KERR: Good! If everybody would stop doing it, there'd be a lot fewer accidents.

BOB: I know.

MR. KERR: You never can tell what the driver in front of you is going to do next.

BOB: Really . . . !

MR. KERR: If all of a sudden he stops, and you're too close, there's no way to stop in time.

BOB: I know. It all happens so fast!

MR. KERR: You're just out of luck, that's all.

BOB: And all of a sudden you've smashed up your front end, ruined your radiator, and . . .

MR. KERR: Bob . . . ? You didn't . . . *did you*?

BOB: Dad . . . believe me, it'll never happen again! I've given up tailgating for good!

MR. KERR: *Bob!* Oh, no . . . !

Questions
1. Why was Bob's father surprised to see him?
2. What is it that Mr. Kerr doesn't like about his son's driving?
3. Why did Bob decide to give up tailgating?
4. What damage did Bob do to the family car?
5. Describe the damage that you think Bob did to the car in front of him.

Correct the statements
1. Mr. Kerr was enjoying the book he was reading.
2. Bob entered his house through the front door.
3. If everybody would start tailgating, there wouldn't be any accidents.

17e/f

e / Summary

Focal Points in this Unit

1. In this unit, we have practiced a small number of the verbs which are followed by the *-ing* form (Gerund) of a verb:

mind	like	stop	keep on
hate	give up	enjoy	

Remember these sentences:
   a. Would you *mind helping* me? Would you *mind not waving* that sign?
   b. Joe *hates washing* dishes.
   c. Fred *does not like being* a soldier.
   d. Frank has had to *give up eating* candy.
   e. *Stop waving* that sign!
   f. I wish you'd *stop saying* that.
   g. I've *given up tailgating* for good!

2. Remember how we sometimes begin a sentence with *I wonder . . .* when we want someone to do something, and we want to be very polite:

   I wonder if you'd mind closing the window.

f / Exercises for Homework

1. Do all the exercises on pages 99, 100 and 102.

2. Complete these sentences:
   a. I've just given up . . .
   b. Why don't you stop . . .
   c. Do you like . . .
   d. Do you really enjoy . . .
   e. We don't mind . . .
   f. I hate . . .
   g. You really ought to give up . . .
   h. Shall I stop . . .
   i. Will you please stop . . .
   j. I wonder if you'd mind . . .

3. Give advice to these people. Use "You'd better give up / stop . . ."
   a. A friend who spends all his money.
   b. A man who is putting on weight.
   c. A light sleeper who always drinks coffee before he goes to bed.
   d. A young girl who always drives very fast.
   e. A student who has an exam next week, but who goes out every evening.

4. **Guided Composition**
   a. Read situation 3 on page 99 again, and then, using the cues, write about this person:
      John Roberts / bank / 3 years // not like / bank teller // In fact . . . // money / suit // also / to work early // other tellers / already there // "I wonder . . . / earlier?" the manager has just asked him.
   b. Read situation 5 on page 99 again, and then write a radio commentator's report of the meeting. Use the patterns and vocabulary in the situation. (Remember, you did one like this in Unit 16.)

5. **Transfer Exercise**
   a. Write 5 true sentences about things you like, enjoy or hate doing.
   b. Write 5 true sentences using *stop* or *give up.*
   Examples:
   I gave up smoking a year ago.

   I stopped studying Physics when I graduated from high school.

1

a. What / Fred / about to do?
b. What / another?
c. Why / Fred / not jump?
d. What / if?

2

a. What / millionaire / ask?
b. she / make up / mind?
c. asking him?

3

a. What / student / ask?
b. What / driver / say?

4

a. What / Jane?
b. When / other secretaries?
c. What / her boss / worried?
d. boss / angry / if?

5

a. Which team / win?
b. What / if / tie?
c. How / players?

1

Fred is about to jump across the stream. One of the other soldiers has just fallen into it. Fred does not want to jump. He is afraid he will fall into it too. He will get soaked if he does. Fred will be very happy when all of this is over.

1. What is Fred about to do?
2. What has just happened?
3. Why doesn't Fred want to jump?
4. Ask and answer these questions:
   a. Fred / soaked / falls
   b. happy / over

2

The old millionaire has just asked the young blonde to marry him. She can't make up her mind. Maybe she will and maybe she won't.

"Will you give me all your money if I marry you?" she is asking him.

1. What has just happened?
2. Will the blonde marry him?
3. What can't she do?
4. What exactly is she asking him?

3

This foreign student does not know New York at all. He has just asked the bus driver to tell him when they get to Central Park. The driver is saying, "Don't worry! I'll tell you when we get there!"

1. Where does the foreign student want to go?
2. What has he just asked the driver to do?
3. What is the driver saying?
4. What do you think was the student's exact question?

4

Jane is working late this evening. The other secretaries left five minutes ago. Jane's boss is leaving too. He is worried about the lights.

"Don't worry! I'll turn them off when I leave," Jane is saying.

He will be very angry if she forgets.

1. What is Jane doing?
2. Why aren't the other secretaries there?
3. What is Jane's boss worried about?
4. What is Jane saying to him?
5. Ask and answer the question:
   boss angry / forgets?

5

There are only two minutes left in this championship football game between Lincoln High and Union High. Union is ahead 21 to 14, but they have not won yet. Lincoln might get another touchdown, and if they do, the game will end in a tie. If that happens, the Union High fans will be very disappointed. The players are tired. They will probably be very happy when the game is over.

1. What is going on here? Which team is winning?
2. What may Lincoln do? Ask and answer: Lincoln win / score?
3. Ask some more questions and answer them:
   a. Lincoln score / a tie
   b. Union fans happy / Lincoln
   c. players happy / over

18b FORMATION AND MANIPULATION

1 Pronunciation

These are contractions: *I'll, he'll, she'll, we'll, they'll* and *it'll.* Notice that these contractions are not used in questions: *Will you give me all your money if I marry you?* (situation 2, page 105).

2

I'll	turn them off	if when	I leave.

Notice that we use *if* when we cannot be sure that the thing is going to happen:
   He will (he'll) get soaked *if* he does (situation 3, page 105).
Notice that we use *when* when we know that the thing is going to happen:
   I'll tell you *when* we get there (situation 3, page 105).

3 Transformations

Make sentences using *when* or *if*.
Examples: Perhaps it will (it'll) rain. He'll get wet.
   He'll get wet if it rains.
   She knows he's arriving. She'll meet him.
   She'll meet him when he arrives.

a. I know I'll see John. I'll tell him then.
b. Perhaps I'll see John. I'll tell him then.
c. Perhaps I'll marry that man. He'll give me $100,000.
d. We know it'll get dark. We'll turn on the lights then.
e. I'm going to bed. I'll turn off the lights then.

4

Will you	give me all your money	if when	I marry you?

5

Yes, I will. (no short form)
No, I won't.

6 Make sentences, ask questions and answer them. Work with someone else. Ask and answer as many questions as you can.

I'll do it	if when	you	come. ask me. pay me $50.

Will you	come be here wait stop	when if	I	ask you? tell you? phone you? see you?

The Man Who Escaped

EPISODE 18

SUMMARY: *Rossi went to the Ringside Club to look for John Kincaid. Antonio, the headwaiter, called Kincaid to tell him some people were asking about him. Then Hooper called Kincaid and told him about the old man and the woman.*

Fletcher did not sleep well that night. He lay awake thinking. Slowly, however, he formed a plan in his mind. He fell asleep around three o'clock.

5 "What are we going to do now?" Marilyn asked in the morning while they were eating breakfast. Fletcher did not answer immediately. He stared into his coffee. He knew he had to make one thing clear to her.

10 "Have you thought about what'll happen to you if the police find you with me?" he suddenly asked. Marilyn looked at him calmly. "We've been over this before, haven't we? Now answer my question," she said.

15 "But you'll be in trouble if anybody finds out you helped me."

"I'll worry about that if and when it happens."

"All right. I'll tell you. But I warn you, if 20 anything goes wrong, you might get hurt, badly hurt!" he told her.

"Go on. I'm listening."

"We're going to try to get Kincaid to come here. That is, if the owner of that shop is 25 Kincaid."

"Get him to come here? How?"

Fletcher began to explain the plan he had in mind.

John Kincaid was cleaning an antique pistol 30 when the phone rang in his shop. He heard a young woman's voice at the other end. "I believe you buy and sell antique weapons," she said.

"Yes, that's right. I'm particularly 35 interested in old firearms."

"My father is too. He has a number of 17th-century pistols and he wants to sell some of them. Would you be interested?"

"Certainly. If you bring them to my shop, 40 I'll look at them and give you a price."

"Well, unfortunately my father isn't well enough to leave the hotel today. Would you mind coming here?" the woman asked.

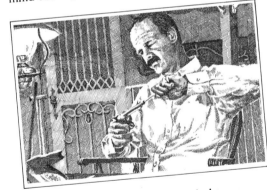

Kincaid managed to answer calmly.

"Well . . . ah . . . my assistant is out to lunch. 45 I'll come over when he comes back. Is that all right?" He wrote down the name of the hotel and hung up. His hands were shaking slightly.

"These must be the people Hooper told me 50 about," he thought. He reached into a drawer and took out a gun. This one was not an antique.

18d FURTHER PRACTICE

1 / Practice Situations

Make one sentence for each of the situations.
Use: "I'll (do) . . . if . . . or: I'll (do) . . .
    when . . ."

SITUATION: Sally is going to arrive at 10:30.
You'll be at the bus station to meet
her.

RESPONSE: **I'll meet her when she arrives.**

SITUATION: It might rain tomorrow.
I'll take my umbrella then.

RESPONSE: **I'll take my umbrella if it rains
tomorrow.**

Situations:

a. Beef is definitely going to go up in price. You'll stop buying so much beef then.
b. It might snow tomorrow. You'll stay at home then.
c. The weather might get better. You'll go out then.
d. You know a telegram is coming. You'll tell me the news then.
e. You are working in the garden. It might rain soon. You'll go indoors then.
f. Bruce is definitely going to phone soon. You'll speak to him then.

2 / Conversation

Peter Freeman has just gotten on a bus. He wants to go to a certain address in a part of the city he is not familiar with. On most American buses you pay as you get on. The amount depends on how far you are going.

DRIVER: How far are you going?
PETER: Orinda Way.
DRIVER: Orinda Way? That's 95 cents.
PETER: Oh, will you tell me when we get there, please?
DRIVER: Okay, but you'll see it yourself if you watch for it. It's only a few stops from here.
OLD MAN: I'll tell you when we get there, young man. That's where I get off too.
PETER: Thank you. I'd appreciate it.
OLD MAN: Don't mention it. These young bus drivers won't give you any help even if you ask politely. It was different when I was young.
PETER: Yes, I'm sure it was.

OLD MAN: And the way these young bus drivers drive is even worse. This one will kill us if he doesn't slow down!
PETER: Yes. I suppose he *is* driving a bit fast.
OLD MAN: Look there. Do you see that traffic light up ahead? We'll turn left when we get to it. Orinda Way's the next stop after that. Why do you want to get off there anyway?
PETER: I want to go to the new community college . . .
OLD MAN: Oh? You'll never find it if you go alone. I'll show you where it is if you carry one of my bags for me.
PETER: Well . . . uh . . . thanks all the same but I'm sure I can find it. I mean, I don't want to put you to any trouble.
OLD MAN: Oh, it's no trouble at all. I have to go past there anyway. We're almost there now. Now, I'll carry this small bag if you take that big one. Hurry up or we'll miss the stop!
PETER: It's . . . it's very heavy.
OLD MAN: In fact, it'll be easier to show you the college if you take both bags. That way I'll have both hands free . . .
PETER: I . . . I . . .
OLD MAN: Oh, don't thank me. I'm always ready to help a stranger!

Questions
1. Where does Peter want to get off? Ask why.
2. What exactly does he say to the driver?
3. What does the driver tell Peter?
4. What does the old man say he will do?
5. What does Peter have to do?

Practice
Explain in class exactly what these phrases mean. Then practice the pronunciation and intonation of the phrases using the teacher or tape recorder as a model:
a. Don't mention it.
b. Thanks all the same.
c. I'm sure I can find it.
d. I don't want to put you to any trouble.

e / Summary

Focal Points in this Unit

1. Remember the important difference between *if* and *when* in sentences like these:
   a. Fred will get soaked *if* he falls into the water.
   b. Fred will be very happy *when* all this is over.
   In **a**, Fred might fall into the water. It is not certain, so we use *if*.
   In **b**, Fred knows that all this will finish soon, so we use *when*.

2. Notice particularly the form of the verb in the *if* or *when* part of the sentence:
   a. Will you give me all your money *if I marry* you?
   b. I'll tell you *when we get* there.

3. The word *if* can come at the beginning or the middle of a sentence. Notice that we use a comma in the sentence only if the *if* comes at the beginning.
   The Union High fans will be very disappointed *if* Lincoln gets another touchdown.
   If Lincoln gets another touchdown, the Union High fans will be very disappointed.

f / Exercises for Homework

1. Put the verbs in parentheses in the correct form. They are all future ideas.
   a. I (be) there when she (arrive).
   b. If you (ask) him politely, he (help) you.
   c. What (happen) to me if I (tell) them?
   d. If gas prices (go up) again, I (stop) driving.
   e. Will you tell me when breakfast (be) ready?
   f. If you (take) the 10:30 bus tomorrow, you'll be in Boston at 12 noon.

2. Put the phrases in this list into the correct column (1 or 3):
   you come / you arrive on time / we'll meet you / I'll be there / the weather is good / I'll be very pleased

1	2	3
	if	

Now write at least 5 sentences from the table you have completed.

3. Guided Composition
You have just moved to a new house in a different town. Write a short letter (about 70 words) to a friend in the town where you used to live inviting him (or her) to your new home for a weekend in the near future. Suggest the bus or train he (or she) might take and where and what time you can meet. Begin your letter like this:
   Dear . . .,
      You know we have just moved into our new house here in . . ., so I am writing to ask . . .
Use these phrases and patterns in your letter:
   I'll meet you . . . if you come on . . . // If you say . . ., we'll go out . . . // We won't be able to . . . // You'll never find it if . . . // It'll be easier to . . . if . . . // You'll be able to tell me . . . when we . . . //

4. Transfer Exercise
Write a number of true sentences about yourself using "I'll . . . if / when . . ."
Examples:
I'll go to the beach this afternoon if the weather is good.

I'll buy a new pair of shoes when I get my check at the end of the week.

1

a. What / girl's father?

b. What / he / at the moment?

c. What / if she doesn't?

2

a. Why / girl's mother angry?

b. What / she / to father?

3

a. What / Joe want?

b. What / Susan want?

c. Why?

d. What / say?

4

a. Where / Fred?

b. sick?

c. sergeant / believe?

d. What / sergeant / do?

5

a. When / Peter / Europe?

b. Who else / on plane?

c. What / at Customs?

6

a. Where / woman?

b. early?

c. What / if director?

d. What / before?

muốn ai làm 1 gì)   (*ra lệnh , bắt buộc*)

Want
Ask   someone *to* do
Tell

Make
Let   someone do   **19a**

(để cho phép)

1

The girl's father wants her to stop playing. He wants her to wash her face and hands and eat dinner. At the moment he is asking her to do these things. If she does not do them, he will make her do them.
1. What does the girl's father want her to stop doing?
2. What else does he want her to do?
3. What is he doing at the moment?
4. What will he do if she does not do these things?

2

The little girl's father told her to stop playing a few seconds ago, but she hasn't stopped yet. The girl's mother has just looked in. She is angry. "Make her stop! Don't let her play any longer!" she is saying to the girl's father.
1. What hasn't the little girl done?
2. What did her father do a few seconds ago?
3. What does the girl's mother think the father should do?
4. What does she think he shouldn't do?

3

Joe wants to read a book but Susan won't let him. She wants him to read something in the paper. It is an advertisement for a better job.
"Put that book down a second and look at this! Why don't you apply for this job?" she is saying.
1. What is it that Susan won't let Joe do?
2. What are the three things she wants him to do (book / paper / the job)?
3. What does she want him to stop doing?

4

Fred is out on a long march. He is not really sick but he wants the sergeant to think he is.
"Let me sit here a while, Sergeant. I feel terrible!" he is saying.
Unfortunately, the sergeant does not believe him. He is going to make Fred get up again. He is going to make him march with the other soldiers.
1. What does Fred want the sergeant to think?
2. Ask why (and answer).
3. What does Fred want the sergeant to do?
4. What exactly is Fred saying?
5. Ask three questions about the sergeant. Use *let* or *make* and begin "Is he going to . . .?"
    a. Fred / up again   c. march
    b. sit there

5

Two months ago, when Peter flew back from Europe, there was a very pretty young woman on the same plane. When Peter went through Customs, they made him open his suitcase. They made him take everything out. They did not make the woman do these things. They let her go through without any trouble.
1. When did this happen?
2. What did they make Peter do?
3. Ask two questions about the woman, beginning "Why didn't they make her . . .?"
4. What did they let the woman do?
5. Ask why they didn't let Peter do this.

6

Here is the same young woman again. She is going into a movie studio in Hollywood. She got up late this morning. The auditions for parts have already started. They started an hour ago. She does not want the director to see her come in. If he does, he might not let her stay. He made her leave once before when she came late for auditions.
1. Why is the woman in a movie studio?
2. Ask two questions about her:
    a. early or late this morning
    b. already started
3. What doesn't she want the director to do? Ask why (and answer).
4. What happened once before?

19b FORMATION AND MANIPULATION

1 Pronunciation

Don't forget to use the weak (unstressed) form of *to* (/ tə /).
Example: The girl's father wants her to (/ tə /) stop playing.

2 Notice the type of word we put in each box:

A	B	C	D	
My boss	wants	me	to work	late this evening.

a. Think of some words of your own to put in box A (*My boss*). Change *wants* to *want* where necessary. Make complete sentences.

b. What other words can we put in box C (*me*)? Make at least six sentences by changing *me* to other words, like *him, us,* etc.

c. Now think of other words to go in box D (*to work*). Make sure they are *to + verb*. Do not use *late this evening*. Again, make complete sentences. (*Example:* **He wants me to finish these letters.**)

d. Finally, change box B. Make sentences with *wanted, ask/asked* and *tell/told*.

3

A	B	C	D
People today	let	their children	do	all kinds of things that children couldn't do before.

a. What are some of these things? Make sentences of your own beginning: "They let them . . ."

b. Are there things you think parents shouldn't let their children do? What are they?

4 Make sentences from this table:

A	B	C	D
He She They	wanted asked 'll tell	me him them John	to	come in. go away. stop playing. help her.
He She	made let	John them		do it. wait.

5

a. Now think of things that your parents wanted you to do when you were young. Make sentences beginning: "They wanted me to . . ."

b. Now ask someone else questions beginning "Did your parents want you to . . .?"

c. What were some of the things your parents made you do?
Make at least five sentences.

The Man Who Escaped
EPISODE 19

SUMMARY: *Marilyn has asked Kincaid to come to their hotel. She told him that her father had some antique pistols he wanted to sell. Kincaid was suspicious and decided to take a gun with him.*

Just before Kincaid left his shop, he decided to call Hooper.

"You told me about an old man and a woman . . . well, they just called. They want 5 me to go to their hotel and look at some antique pistols," he said nervously.

"Well, what do you want me to do about it?" Hooper asked sarcastically. "You have a gun, don't you? There isn't much an old man 10 and a woman can do to you," he added.

Kincaid could not understand why Hooper was so casual about it. He got into his car and drove to the hotel.

"Perhaps the old man really does want me to 15 look at his pistols," he thought. He patted the gun in his pocket. It made him feel safer.

He felt even safer when Marilyn opened the door. She was slim, almost delicate looking. "Good afternoon," he said. "I'm John Kin-20 caid. You called earlier." She smiled. "I hope I haven't put you to any trouble. However, I'm sure you'll decide we haven't made you come all this way for nothing," she said pleasantly, and led him into the room. Kincaid glanced 25 suspiciously at the old man sitting in the corner. At first he seemed harmless enough, but there was something familiar about the man's face that made Kincaid look more closely at him.

30 "I'll get the pistols," Marilyn said. Kincaid stayed where he was, where he could see everything and where nobody could come in behind him. The old man did not move.

"Are you a collector too?" Kincaid asked. 35 The old man simply nodded. The woman brought out a large black case. "They're all in here," she said. "If you'll come over here, to the table, we can look at them. My father doesn't really want anyone else to have them, 40 but I'm afraid we have no choice. It's a question of money."

Kincaid kept his eyes on the old man's face as he walked towards the table. He was halfway there when the old man raised his head 45 slightly. The sudden movement made Kincaid stop. The more he looked at that face, the more suspicious he became. Suddenly it dawned on him. He looked from one to the other. They were both waiting expectantly for him to come 50 closer. It was the old man's nose and lips that made Kincaid think of Fletcher. He reached for his gun.

19d FURTHER PRACTICE

1 / Invention Exercise

1. MODEL: I can't go out tonight.
    Someone wants me to do something.
    CUE: my mother / some letters
    RESPONSE: **I can't go out tonight. My mother wants me to write some letters.**

    Cues:
    a. My boss / some extra work
    b. My teacher / a composition
    c. My father / his car
    d. My mother / the kitchen
    e. My kids / a bedtime story
    f. My parents / to a concert
    g. My friend / a special program on TV
    h. My younger brother / his homework

2. MODEL: Would you please $\begin{Bmatrix} \text{ask} \\ \text{tell} \end{Bmatrix}$ someone to do something?
    CUE: Mary / the kitchen door
    RESPONSE: **Would you please tell Mary to close the kitchen door?**
    or: **Would you please ask Mary to open the kitchen door?**

    Cues:
    a. Jane / the window
    b. that student / the lights on
    c. Jane / me before she goes
    d. Mr. Smith / my office
    e. them / more quietly
    f. that boy / here
    g. him / my bike
    h. her / the 1977 reports

2 / Conversation

It's a beautiful spring day. Joe is sitting in his yard at home reading a murder mystery.

SUSAN: Joe? Do you think you could come into the kitchen for a second? There's something I'd like you to look at.

JOE: What? Just let me finish this chapter and I'll be right there.

SUSAN: Would you mind coming right away, please? It's the washing machine. It's making a funny noise. I want you to listen to it. I'm worried.

JOE: Oh, no! Not again. (Joe is in the kitchen now. He has to shout above a loud whirring and pumping noise.) It's the pump, that's what it is.

SUSAN: I can't hear you. Let me turn the machine off!

JOE: The pump isn't working right. What do you want me to do about it?

SUSAN: Fix it, of course. You don't think I made you come in here for nothing, do you?

JOE: But I'm not a mechanic. Why don't you call the store where we bought the thing? Ask them to fix it!

SUSAN: Are you sure that's what you want me to do?

JOE: Of course I'm sure! Why do you ask?

SUSAN: Because the last time they came you got very upset.

JOE: I did . . .?

SUSAN: Yes. It was a small question of money. Don't you remember? The men were only here half an hour but they still charged $20 for the service call. You didn't like that at all.

JOE: Oh. Hmm . . . yes, I remember now. Okay, I'll try to fix it myself.

Questions
1. Why is Susan worried about the washing machine?
2. What exactly does she want Joe to do about it? Ask why.
3. What does he want her to do?
4. What happened the last time something went wrong with the machine?
5. When Susan first asks him to come in, Joe wants to finish the chapter he is reading; what does he say to Susan?

e / Summary

Focal Points in this Unit

1. Remember the form of the verb which follows the verbs *want*, *ask* and *tell:*

   want / ask / tell + *to* + *verb*

   He *wants* her *to wash* her hands.

   Why don't you *ask* them *to repair* it?

   He *told* her *to stop* playing.

2. Remember the form of the verb which follows *make* and *let:*

   make / let + *verb* (without *to*)

   They *made* him *open* his suitcases.

   They *let* her *go* through without any trouble.

3. There is an important difference in meaning between *make* and *let* as we have used them in this unit.

   Make someone do means "force or cause someone to do."

   Let someone do means "allow someone to do."

4. Remember also the form of the personal pronoun we use in patterns 1 and 2 above: *me, you, him, her, it, us, you, them.*

f / Exercises for Homework

1. Do all the exercises on pages 111, 112 and 114.

2. Choose the correct word to put in the blanks:
   a. He wanted . . . to tell him the time.
      (my / mine / me)
   b. I asked . . . to wash the car yesterday.
      (he / him / his)
   c. Don't let . . . take the books away.
      (they / them / their)
   d. Don't ask . . . to make a pot of coffee.
      (her / hers / she)
   e. She made . . . do more work. (we / us / our)

3. Complete these sentences, using the patterns we have practiced in the unit:
   a. She won't let . . .
   b. Why don't you ask . . .
   c. I hope he doesn't make . . .
   d. If you've got the time, I'd like . . .
   e. Do you really want . . .

4. **Guided Composition**
   Read the second part of the Episode (lines 17-41) again carefully, and then tell about Kincaid's experience as Kincaid might have written it down later. Begin like this:
   "The woman told me that she would get the pistols. I stayed where I could see everything and where nobody could come behind me. I asked the old man if he was a collector too, but he . . ."

5. **Transfer Exercise**
   Write a number of true sentences about yourself using this model:
   I didn't want to do it myself, so I
       asked someone else to do it.
       told someone else to do it.
       made someone else do it.
   Examples:
   I didn't want to do the shopping myself, so I made my sister do it.

   I didn't want to see him myself, so I asked my friend to see him.

1

a. Why / man surprised?
b. What / man saying?
(sure / one baby)
(never / twins!)

2

a. When / Sheriff / saloon?
b. Who / at the bar?
c. Why / Jones / shoot?
d. What / man really?

3

a. When / millionaire / "a little present"?
b. What / he / just?
c. Why / she / surprised?

4

a. Where / Peter / tell / girlfriend / take?
b. Peter / know / crowded?
c. What / girl think?
d. she / stay?

thought
had no idea — *trí không ngờ*.
was sure
never dreamed   someone   **was going to do**   **20a**
                            something   **was going to happen**

1

This man's wife has just had twins. Seven months ago the doctor said she was going to have a baby. The man is very surprised. "I was sure we were going to have only one baby. I never dreamed we were going to have twins!" he is saying.

1. What has just happened?
2. Why is the man so surprised?
3. Ask if the doctor knew.
4. What is the man saying?
5. Now correct the false statements like this:
   Cue: The woman has just had a baby.
   Response: No, she has just had twins.
   a. The doctor told them she was going to have twins.
   b. The man knew she was going to have twins.

2

This is a scene from a cowboy movie. Sheriff Wyatt Jones came into the Crazy Cactus Saloon a few seconds ago. A stranger was standing at the bar when Jones came in. He put his hand in his pocket and Jones shot him dead. "I thought he was going to take out a gun. I thought he was going to shoot me. That's why I shot him first!" Jones is saying. In fact, the man was only going to look at his watch.

1. What was the stranger doing when Jones came in?
2. What did the stranger do?
3. What did Jones do? Ask why.
4. What was the stranger really going to do?
5. Correct the statements as before:
   a. Jones knew the man.
   b. He shot him because he did not like him.
   c. He knew he was going to take out his watch.

3

nhà triệu phú

A few weeks before Christmas, the old millionaire told his young girlfriend that he was going to give her "a little present." It is Christmas morning now. He has just given her the present. In fact, he has not given her "a little present" at all. He has just given her a large diamond ring. The girl is very surprised. "I never realized you were going to give me a diamond ring. I thought you were going to give me a watch, or something like that!" she is saying.

1. What did he tell her a few weeks ago?
2. What day is it now and what has he just done?
3. Why is the girl so surprised?
4. Correct the statements as before:
   a. The girl thought he was going to give her a car.
   b. The girl realized two weeks ago he was going to give her the ring.

realize (vt) thực biết, được biết

4

A few hours ago Peter told one of his girlfriends he was going to take her to a "quiet, elegant restaurant." They have just come in. "I had no idea it was going to be so crowded," Peter is saying. The girl thought it was going to be an elegant place. She does not find it very elegant at all. She wants to go somewhere else.

1. What did Peter tell the girl earlier?
2. What is he saying now?
3. What did the girl think before she came?
4. Correct the statements as before:
   a. The girl finds the place elegant.
   b. Peter knew it was going to be like this.
   c. The girl wants to stay.

20b FORMATION AND MANIPULATION

1 Stress

Remember to use the weak (unstressed) forms of *was* and *were* when speaking. But remember that the full forms are used in short answers: Yes, I *was*. / Yes, they *were*.

2 Notice the construction:

	A	B	C
I didn't know	you he she they	were	going to do that.

What changes do we have to make in box B when we use words like *he, she*, etc., instead of *you*?

A	B	C
I never dreamed	you were	going to do that.

a. What other phrases can you think of to go in box A? Make complete sentences.
b. Make more sentences by replacing *you were* in box B.
c. Think of some things you didn't know were going to happen. Make sentences beginning *I had no idea / I didn't know /* etc., with at least six other things to go in box C.

3 Notice the construction:

A	B	C	D	E
The doctor said	she	was going to	have	a baby.

a. Think of other words to replace *the doctor*.
b. Think of other words to replace those in boxes B, D and E.

4 Read this. Notice the question and answer that come from it. Then, with someone else, do the same with the other sentences.

> Jane went out at 8:00 without an umbrella. It began to rain at 9:00.
> Question: **Did she know it was going to rain?**
> Answer: **No, I don't think so, because she didn't take her umbrella.**

a. Jane ran to the bus stop but the bus came late.
b. Susan put on her light summer clothes. It got very cold later.
c. Peter's girlfriend put on her best clothes. He took her to a very cheap restaurant.
d. The stranger did not even look at Sheriff Jones. Jones shot him dead.

The Man Who Escaped
EPISODE 20

SUMMARY: *Kincaid has come to Marilyn's and Fletcher's hotel. He looked at Fletcher carefully and finally realized who he was. He has just pulled out a gun.*

When Kincaid pulled out the gun, Marilyn was standing between him and Fletcher. She could see he was almost hysterical and was probably going to shoot.

5 "It's you, Fletcher!" he burst out and went closer. Marilyn was standing in his way now and he put out a hand to push her away.

Fletcher could hardly believe his eyes. One minute Kincaid was pointing a gun at him and 10 the next minute he was lying on the floor, gasping for breath. Marilyn had thrown him over her shoulder. "I once played a policewoman in a film and I had to learn some judo," she said rather casually and looked down at Kincaid. 15 Fletcher stared at her in surprise. He picked up the gun that Kincaid had dropped, still looking at Marilyn in disbelief.

Kincaid groaned. He, too, could hardly believe what had happened. It all seemed 20 incredible. He shook his head. He decided it was probably all a nightmare, a horrible dream. He was sure that he was going to wake up at any moment, safe in his own bed. He blinked his eyes several times, hoping that Marilyn and 25 Fletcher were somehow going to disappear. He blinked again, but when he opened his eyes, they were still there.

"And now that you're here, perhaps you wouldn't mind answering some questions," 30 Fletcher said. Kincaid groaned again.

"Questions? What questions?" he mumbled. He was still in a daze.

"I want you to tell me everything that happened that evening you sent me to 35 Philadelphia," Fletcher said in a low voice. Kincaid now realized that it was not a dream. For a moment he thought he was going to be sick.

"I don't know what you're talking about," 40 Kincaid answered.

"I think you do," Fletcher said.

"You can't make me tell you anything!" Kincaid waited to see what Fletcher was going to do next. He could not take his eyes off the 45 gun in Fletcher's hand.

"I'll give you five seconds to begin answering my questions. Then I'll shoot," was all that Fletcher said.

"You couldn't shoot me like that, in cold 50 blood!"

"Couldn't I?" Fletcher answered, and pulled back the safety catch. The gun was now ready to fire. He began counting.

20d FURTHER PRACTICE

1 / Invention Exercise

Make sentences with:
"I thought he / she / it was going to . . ."
"I had no idea we / you / they were going to . . ."

CUE: coffee shop / so crowded
RESPONSE: **I had no idea the coffee shop was going to be so crowded.**

CUE: work early today
RESPONSE: **I thought you were going to leave work early today.**
or: **I thought they were going to get to work early today.**

Cues:
a. beautiful yesterday
b. program / so uninteresting
c. tests / so difficult
d. the bill himself
e. in bed yesterday
f. her a present
g. concert / so good
h. a party tomorrow night
i. movie / so bad
j. a trip to Canada this year

2 / Conversation

In the conversation in Unit 13, Joe Freeman described an accident he saw. A white Ford shot out in front of a blue car. In this conversation we hear the two lawyers questioning the driver of the blue car.

1ST LAWYER: Please tell the court exactly what happened.

DRIVER: Certainly. I was driving home along Harbor Boulevard. I was just going to slow down when I saw a white Ford approaching the corner. I was sure he was going to wait on the side street until I drove past. I had no idea he was going to shoot out in front of me.

1ST LAWYER: In other words, the driver of the white Ford shot out without any warning, is that right?

DRIVER: Exactly. It was completely unexpected.

1ST LAWYER: And you had no idea this was going to happen?

DRIVER: No! None whatsoever!

1ST LAWYER: Thank you.

2ND LAWYER: Hmm . . . you say you were going to slow down when the accident happened, is that right?

DRIVER: Yes, I was about to slow down.

2ND LAWYER: I see. I suppose you were going pretty fast.

DRIVER: No, not at all! I was going 30, that's all.

2ND LAWYER: Well, why were you going to slow down, then? That suggests to me, and I'm sure to the court as well, that you were going too fast in the first place.

DRIVER: No! The reason I was going to slow down was very simple. I was going to turn at the next corner.

2ND LAWYER: Really? Why?

DRIVER: Because I live there, that's why!

Questions

1. What did the driver of the blue car think the other driver was going to do?
2. What did the other driver do? Ask if the driver of the blue car knew this.
3. What makes the 2nd lawyer think he was going very fast?
4. Ask and answer why he was going to slow down.

Recall

Without looking at the text, see if you can remember these parts of the conversation:

1ST LAWYER: any idea / happen?
DRIVER: whatsoever
2ND LAWYER: say / slow down / right?
DRIVER: Yes / down.
2ND LAWYER: pretty fast?
DRIVER: 30
2ND LAWYER: slow down then?
DRIVER: at the next corner / live

e / Summary

Focal Points in this Unit

1. These are the main patterns we have learned in this unit:

   a. I thought
   b. I had no idea
   c. I was sure   + (that)
   d. I never dreamed
   e. I never realized

   he was going to do that.

   they were going to come.

   Note that in everyday conversation, we nearly always leave out the word *that*.

2. Remember how we use *was / were going to* after *said* and *told*:

   a. The doctor said she was going to have a baby.
   b. He told his young girlfriend that he was going to give her a little present.

3. Remember the other pattern with *going to* used by the driver in the Conversation on page 120:

   "I was just going to slow down when I saw a white Ford . . ."

   Notice the position of the word *just*.

f / Exercises for Homework

1. Do all the exercises on pages 117, 118 and 120.

2. Complete these sentences using *was / were going to* . . .

   a. We didn't really know . . .
   b. The doctor didn't think . . .
   c. The driver never dreamed . . .
   d. Peter never realized . . .
   e. Joe was sure . . .
   f. We all thought . . .
   g. The girl had no idea . . .

3. Do you remember the pattern . . . *so (well / fast / badly, etc.) that* . . .? We practiced it in Unit 7. Look at these 2 sentences. They combine *so . . . that . . .* and *thought*, etc. . . . *was going to . . .*

   He *drove so fast that I thought he was going to have* an accident.

   She *played so beautifully that I was sure she was going to win* a prize.

   Now write more sentences like this using the cues:

   a. dangerously / job
   b. slowly / late
   c. badly / walk out
   d. carelessly / the football game
   e. fast / early

4. **Guided Composition**

   Write a short story about a day that turned out badly. Begin with this sentence:

   When I woke up, the sun was shining and I thought it was going to be a beautiful day.

   Then use these phrases for the beginnings of some of the sentences:

   It was the first day . . . // As soon as . . . // When I went into the garage . . . // The tire . . . // I never realized . . . // Two hours later . . . // She was still waiting . . . // Just then it began . . . // It was still raining . . . // The weather was so . . . //

5. **Transfer Exercise**

   Look at the patterns in point 1 of the *Focal Points in this Unit*. Use each of them to write 2 true sentences about yourself, the weather, this lesson, etc.

1

a. Why / policeman / man / station?
b. Who / corner?
c. When / arrest?

2

a. How long ago / accident / happen?
b. What / Peter / see?
c. Why / policeman / man / station?

3

a. Who / Jane / bank?
b. Why / night deposit box?
c. What / man?
d. Jane's answer?

4

a. Who / ask / questions?
b. How long ago?
c. What / Jane / when / man?
d. ever before then?

5

a. Who / Bruce's office?
b. done to his desk?
   letters?
   money?
   lamp?
c. Why / run away?

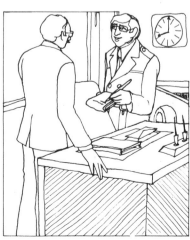

6

a. Who / ask / questions?
b. Bruce / see burglars?
c. What / Bruce / see?
d. What sort / mess / they?

1

One car has run into another. A policeman is taking one of the drivers to the police station because, just after the accident, the man got out of his car and hit the other driver. Peter has just come around the corner. The policeman arrested the man a few seconds ago.

1. What has one car done?
2. Ask what the policeman is doing.
3. Ask why.
4. What has Peter just done?
5. What did the policeman do a few seconds ago?

2

Peter is talking about what he saw a few hours ago. "I saw there had been an accident. One car had run into another. When I got there, a policeman was taking one driver to the station. The man had hit the other driver. That's why the policeman had arrested him."

xảy ra sau

rất ra trước

1. What does Peter say that shows he did not see the accident happen?
2. What had one car done?
3. What was the policeman doing? Why?
4. What had the policeman done?

3

Jane's boss has sent her to the bank with a lot of money, but the bank was closed. That is why she has put the money in the night deposit box. A man has suddenly appeared. "I want your money!" he has just shouted.

"But I've put it in the night deposit box!" Jane is saying. She is very frightened.

1. What has Jane's boss done?
2. What has Jane done with the money? Why?
3. What has the man just shouted?
4. Why can't Jane give him the money?

4

A policeman is asking Jane questions.
   "When did all this happen?"
   "Half an hour ago. I'd just put the money in the night deposit box when I saw him."
   "Had you ever seen the man before then?"
   "No, I hadn't. He was a total stranger."

1. What is happening now?
2. Why didn't the man get the money?
3. Why didn't Jane take the money into the bank itself?
4. Correct the statements:
   a. She was going to put the money into the night deposit box when she saw the man.
   b. She knew the man.

5

Burglars have broken into Bruce's office. They have emptied his desk, thrown all his letters on the floor and have taken most of the money from the safe. They have also smashed the lamp on his desk. They are running away because they have just heard Bruce in the outside office.

1. What have they done to his desk?
2. What else have they done?
3. What are they doing now? Why?
4. Correct the statements:
   a. They have taken all the money.
   b. They have left his letters in the desk.

6

A policeman is asking Bruce questions.
   "Did you see the burglars?"
   "No, they'd already run away when I came in."
   "What did you see when you came in?"
   "Nothing, except what they'd done. They'd made a terrible mess."

1. Why didn't Bruce see the burglars?
2. Make as many sentences as you can beginning "Bruce saw they had . . ."
3. Ask questions beginning:
   "Had they . . . when he got there?"
   Answer "Yes, they had. / No, they hadn't."

21b FORMATION AND MANIPULATION

1 Pronunciation
Remember that the word *had* has the form *'d* in contractions.

2 Study this example:

A	B	C	D	E
She had (She'd)	already just	left	when he	called.

a. Think of some words to replace *she* in box A. (Remember that you can use words like *Peter* and *the bus*.)
b. Now, think of some words to replace *left* in box C.
c. Now, think of some words to replace *called* in box E.
d. Using the words you have thought of, write or say ten sentences using *already* or *just*.

3 Study this table:

Jane hadn't	gotten up washed the dishes eaten finished her work gotten dressed	when Jim got there.

a. Use this table for this conversation. (Talk with another person.)
   A: Why did Jim have to wait for Jane?   B: Because she hadn't . . .
b. Use the table again to ask questions like this. (Talk with someone else and tell him or her to take B's part.)
   A: Had Jane . . . when Jim got there?   B: No, she hadn't. That's why he had to wait.

4 Look at this conversation:
A: What had happened when she got there?   B: They'd already left.
Make other conversations like this with the person sitting next to you using the following cues:

a. A: got there   B: left
b. A: arrived   B: phoned
c. A: saw it   B: finished
d. A: went in   B: started
e. A: rain started   B: game begun
f. A: man arrived   B: she gone

Now, do the same thing again using the word *just* instead of *already*.

The Man Who Escaped
EPISODE 21

SUMMARY: *Marilyn threw Kincaid on the floor. Fletcher grabbed Kincaid's gun and told him he would kill him if he did not answer his questions. Fletcher is going to count to five before he shoots.*

"But I know nothing!" Kincaid protested.

Fletcher had already raised the gun and simply said, "One!"

Kincaid said nothing.

5 "Two!" Fletcher brought the gun closer.

"You can't frighten me!" Kincaid shouted.

"Three!" Kincaid saw Fletcher had already taken aim.

"How can I tell you something I don't
10 know?" Kincaid demanded.

"Four!" Kincaid watched Fletcher's finger beginning to press the trigger.

"All right, all right, I'll tell you anything you want, but first put that gun down!" Kincaid
15 gasped.

Fletcher's mind went back to the time, five years earlier, when both he and Kincaid had been officers in the same Army Intelligence unit in Washington. Kincaid had been
20 Fletcher's superior. Several top military documents had disappeared and they were both trying to find out who had taken them.

One night, on Kincaid's orders, Fletcher had gone to an address in Philadelphia. Kincaid had
25 told him he would meet a possible informer there. When he arrived, three men grabbed him from behind. They had forced whiskey down his throat and then hit him over the head.

When he came to, he was back in his car, but
30 it had crashed into a tree. The police had already arrived. They thought that Fletcher had gotten drunk and lost control of his car. They

had found several documents marked "Top Secret" in his car. Fletcher swore he had never
35 seen them before. The FBI also found that Fletcher had apparently deposited more than $10,000 in his checking account a few weeks before. Fletcher had known nothing about the money. The bank said the checks had arrived
40 by mail, with Fletcher's signature on them. Nobody believed Fletcher's story. Everybody believed that he had sold military secrets. Kincaid denied he had ever told Fletcher to go to Philadelphia. This is what Fletcher wanted to
45 ask questions about now.

21d FURTHER PRACTICE

1 / For Comprehension

Read this newspaper report and then answer the questions:

GOLD ON THE KLONDIKE!

San Francisco, September 20, 1897. A small group of miners arrived here yesterday with news of a fabulous gold strike in the Yukon Territory. Carrying gold worth nearly $2 million, the miners had amazing stories about their experiences.

The miners said they had been living in Alaska for over a year when they got news of the discovery of gold on the Klondike River. They said it had taken nearly five months for news of this gold strike to reach them, and that most of them had left for the Klondike immediately.

On their trip back to San Francisco, the miners said they had traveled over 500 miles by water. Most of the trip was extremely hazardous. They said several boats had capsized when they entered swift currents in the Yukon River, and that several miners had lost their lives when their boats hit rocks.

Most people here are predicting that thousands of men will be leaving San Francisco soon to answer this call of gold on the Klondike.

a. How long had the miners been living in Alaska when they got news of the gold strike?
b. What did most of them do when they heard about the gold strike?
c. What were some of the hazards the miners faced on the trip?
d. Cover the text and write down what the miners said about the Yukon River. (Cues: boats / capsized / swift currents // miners / lost lives / boats / rocks //)

2 / Conversation

Jane Nelson has just gone into her boss's office. Jane had just started typing a letter when her boss called her to come to his office.

MR. ELLIS: Come in and sit down, Jane.
JANE: Thank you. I was just typing your letter to Mr. Drummond. I know you want it to go out this morning . . .

MR. ELLIS: Oh, fine. This won't take long. I want to talk to you about your job.
JANE: (nervously) Is there something wrong, Mr. Ellis?
MR. ELLIS: (laughing) No, not at all. Everything's fine. But I'm making some plans for increasing our staff, and I wanted to get your reaction to the ideas I have.
JANE: Oh, I see. (smiling) I hope your plans include another secretary . . .
MR. ELLIS: Well, yes, as a matter of fact, they do. I realize the workload has been pretty heavy for the last few months.
JANE: Yes, it's been pretty hectic.
MR. ELLIS: How long have you been with us, Jane? Hasn't it been almost a year?
JANE: A little more than a year. Thirteen months to be exact. I hope you don't remember the problems I had when I first started.
MR. ELLIS: Problems? What do you mean?
JANE: Oh, I was always late, and my typing was pretty bad . . .
MR. ELLIS: Oh, yes, I remember. But that didn't last long. Anyway, we need to hire another secretary and then I would like to have you work as my executive secretary. How would you react to that?
JANE: In other words, there would be somebody else to handle Mr. Taylor's correspondence. Is that right?
MR. ELLIS: That's right. You would only be responsible for my correspondence.
JANE: I'd like that.
MR. ELLIS: Good! You'll get a raise, of course, and you will have your own office.
JANE: That's fine. I'm sure it will be easier to get things done without constant interruptions in the outer office.

Questions

1. What had Jane just started doing when her boss called her?
2. How long has Jane had her job?
3. What did Jane say she used to do when she first started working there?
4. Why did Mr. Ellis say he was going to raise Jane's salary?
5. What did Jane say about having a private office?

21e/f

e / Summary

Focal Points in this Unit

. In this unit, we have studied and practiced the Past Perfect tense (*had done*). When we use *had done*, we are concerned with what someone *had already done* or what *had already happened before we got there* or *before we came in*, etc.
Examples:
When I got there, I saw there *had been* an accident.
They *had run* away when I came in.
We often make this even more obvious by using a phrase like *by then* or *by the time . . .*
Example:
By the time I got there, the burglars *had already escaped.*

. Remember the negative form:
She *hadn't seen* the movie before.
and the question form:
Had you ever seen the man before then?
and the short answers:
Yes, I had / No, I hadn't, etc.

/ Exercises for Homework

. Do all the exercises on pages 123, 124 and 126.

. Supply the correct *had done* form of the verb in parentheses:
   a. When I went back to the store, they (sell) the book I wanted.
   b. She (visit) Canada only twice before she went there this year.
   c. As soon as they (go), I went straight to bed.
   d. When we got to the station, we found that the 8 o'clock train (already leave).
   e. When the police got to the bank, the burglar (already escape).
   f. I spoke to the woman because I thought I (meet) her somewhere before.
   g. Laura woke up with a terrible headache because she and Bruce (stay out) late the night before.

3. Look at these two sentences:
   I had never been to Europe before I went there last year.
   She had never seen the Lincoln Memorial before she visited Washington, D.C. last month.
   Now write 5 sentences like this yourself.
   Use these verbs: eat, stay, drink, fly, visit.

4. **Guided Composition**
   a. Read situations 5 and 6 on page 123 again, and then write a short newspaper article (about 60 words) about the robbery:
   Here is the headline:
   BURGLARS BREAK INTO PRESIDENT'S OFFICE
   And begin your article:
   At about 7:20 yesterday morning, burglars broke into the office of Bruce Foster, president of the Foster Shoe Company. When Mr. Foster arrived at about 7:30, he found . . .
   b. Read situations 1 and 2 on page 123 again, and then write the conversation in court one or two days later between a lawyer and Peter. The policeman had taken Peter's name and address as a witness, and Peter had to appear in court. (Remember you read two Conversations like this before, one on page 78 and the other on page 120.)
   Begin like this:
   LAWYER: Now Mr. Freeman, would you please tell the court what you saw when you arrived on the scene of the accident?

5. **Transfer Exercise**
   Write true sentences about things that happened to you or another member of your family or a friend yesterday. Include a *had done* idea at the same time. Here are two examples:
   When I got home last night, the rest of the family had already had dinner.

   I had just gone out in the yard to work yesterday afternoon when it started to rain.

1

a. What / in grass?
b. Why / not run?
c. What / they / if?

2

a. What / attendant / say?
b. Joe's question?
c. more expensive

3

a. What / Peter / say?
b. Why / Joe / use it?

4

a. What / 2 men?
b. Why / difficult?
c. What / both men / say?
   (the job?)
   (these axes?)

5

a. What / not understand?
b. Why / not / job?

6

a. Who / live / house?
b. home / better / i[f]
   grass?
   gate?
   bushes?

1

These people do not know there is a snake in the grass. If they knew, they would probably start screaming and the man would drop his sandwich. If the man had a gun, he could shoot the snake.

1. Why don't the people get up and run now?
2. What would they all do if they knew?
3. Ask and answer the same type of question about:
   a. the man   b. the woman
4. Why can't the man shoot the snake?
5. Now make a sentence: if / a gun / shoot.

2

"If I were you, I'd use Super. Your car would go faster if you did," the gas station attendant said just a minute ago.
   "Would it really?" Joe asked.
   "Yes, it would! Definitely!"
   "But wouldn't it be more expensive?"
   "No, it wouldn't!" the attendant is saying.

1. What did the attendant say he would do if he were Joe? Ask why. (answer)
2. What was Joe's first question?
3. What was the answer and what did Joe ask then?
4. What is the attendant's answer?

3

Peter has just said, "Would it be all right if I borrowed your car this evening? It'd help me a lot if I could use it." Joe would let him use it if he did not need it himself. He is saying, "Unfortunately, I need it myself this evening. I'd let you have it otherwise."

1. Ask and answer why Peter wants to borrow Joe's car.
2. What are the exact words of his question?
3. What is Joe's answer?
4. Ask and answer a question beginning "Would Joe . . . if . . . ?"

4

These two men are trying to cut down a very large tree. Their electric saw is broken. Their axes are not very sharp. "The job would be easy if that saw weren't broken!" one man has just said.
   "These axes would be all right if they were a little sharper!" the other is saying.

1. What are these men doing?
2. Why is it so difficult?
3. Ask and answer the questions:
   a. easy / saw
   b. easy / axes sharper

5

"I can't understand why I can't find a job!" this man is saying. He would probably find one if he got a haircut, shaved off his beard, bought a new suit, put on a clean shirt and polished his shoes.

1. What is the man saying?
2. What do you think he should do?
3. Ask and answer questions beginning "Would he find a job if . . . ?"

6

Two very old people live here. The house would look much better if they painted it, cut the grass, fixed the gate and planted a few trees and bushes. They would probably do this if they weren't so old and if they had a little more money.

1. What kind of people live here?
2. Ask questions beginning: "Do you think the house would . . . if . . . ?"
3. Now ask and answer two questions beginning: "What would they do if . . . ?" (money / old)

22b FORMATION AND MANIPULATION

---

1 Pronunciation
The word *would* has the form *'d* in contractions.
Examples: If I could come, I would tell you.   If she wanted to, she would tell you what happened.
     If I could come, I'd tell you.   If she wanted to, she'd tell you what happened.

---

2 Look at these sentences, then repeat them:
  If they knew, they would start screaming.   Would it be all right if I borrowed your car?
  Your car would go faster if you bought some.   If the man had a gun, he could shoot the snake.
  Questions:
  a. What do you notice about sentences that begin   c. Does it make any difference if the sentence is a
   with *If*?   question?
  b. Now, what about sentences that don't begin   d. So, what can you say about *If* and the comma?
   with *If*?

3

A	B	C	D	E	F	G
If	the man	had a gun	,	he	could shoot	the snake.

  a. Look at the situations on page 129 and find words to replace those in boxes B, C, E, F and G.
  b. Now, make at least ten sentences from the new words you have found in exercise **a**.
  c. Now, practice starting sentences with boxes E, F and G and finishing with A, B and C.

4

a.

What could	he	do	if	he	had a gun?

b.

He	could	shoot	the snake.

Look at the answers you found for exercise **3 b** and use them to make questions and answers like those above.
Example:
a. **What would you do if it rained?**   b. **I would (I'd) go home.**

5

A	B	C
If I were you,	I'd	use Super.

NOTE: We use this form to give advice.
Look at the situations on page 129. Give advice to all of the people.

6

A	B	C
Would it be all right if	I	borrowed your car?

  a. Change the words in boxes B and C. Use words like these in box C: used the phone, arrived late, used the
   bathroom, came in now, saw her, etc.
  b. Think of other phrases to put in box C. (Look at the situations on page 129; you may find some help there.)

The Man Who Escaped
EPISODE 22

SUMMARY: *Fletcher is pointing a gun at Kincaid. Kincaid has agreed to tell Fletcher everything.*

For a moment Fletcher wanted to pull the trigger. He found it difficult not to hate Kincaid. Because of him, he had given up four years of freedom. Because of him, everybody
5 thought he was a spy. But he knew that Kincaid was his only chance to prove he was innocent, and he knew if he killed him, he would lose that chance.

"Let's start at the beginning . . . when you
10 sent me to Philadelphia that night," Fletcher said in a flat, cold voice.

"That was Hooper's idea. I had nothing to do with it."

"And who is Hooper?" Fletcher demanded.
15 "He sells government secrets to any foreign country that's interested. He's the one that framed you. He made me give him information. I didn't want to!"

"Made you? How did he make you?"
20 Fletcher asked.

Kincaid stared down at the floor for several seconds before he answered.

"He knew things about me. He said he would tell the FBI if I didn't help him."

25 "What sort of things?"

Again, Kincaid hesitated before answering.

"I stole a lot of money a few years ago. Hooper knew about it."

There were only a few more things Fletcher
30 wanted to know. "Why did you involve me in all this?"

"The FBI suspected someone. Hooper wanted to make them think you were the spy. He knew they would if they found you dead in
35 the car with all kinds of secret military documents in it."

"Dead?"

"Hooper thought the crash would kill you," Kincaid said.

40 "A pity it didn't. You'd still be safe if I were dead!"

Kincaid swallowed and stared at the floor.

"And why aren't you still in the army? You'd be a lot more useful to Hooper if you
45 were," Fletcher went on.

"It became too dangerous. Anyway, he still uses me."

"How?" Fletcher asked.

"We hide microfilms of secret documents in
50 the antique weapons I send overseas. The people we send them to pretend to be foreign collectors."

Fletcher had one last question. It was the most important. "Where's Hooper now?"

22d FURTHER PRACTICE

1 / Invention Exercise

Write sentences with "If . . . (did) . . . would (do) . . .":

CUE: that movie / it
RESPONSE: **If you saw that movie, you'd enjoy it.**
or: **If they went to see that movie, they'd enjoy it.**

Cues:
a. by bus / to work earlier
b. that house / some flowers and trees
c. my car / on time
d. a haircut / a job
e. Super / much better
f. less / more money
g. better meals / healthier
h. a car / you to the stadium
i. more carefully / fewer mistakes
j. enough money / trip this summer

2 / Conversation

Bruce's secretary has told him she would like to see him about something personal. She has just come into his office.

BRUCE: Sit down, Miss Bradley. It's something personal, you said?
MISS BRADLEY: Yes. You see, I'm going to get married next month and . . .
BRUCE: Get married? I didn't know that. Congratulations!
MISS BRADLEY: Thank you, but I'm afraid it means I've got to quit my job. I'd like to leave at the end of the month.
BRUCE: Really? I'm very sorry to hear that. Do you intend to stop working altogether, then?
MISS BRADLEY: Oh, no! We want to save up enough to buy a house and we wouldn't be able to do that if I stopped working right away. And it isn't that I don't like my job here either. I'd stay if Terry, that's my fiance, weren't Canadian.
BRUCE: Canadian? I'm sorry, I don't understand. What's that got to do with it?
MISS BRADLEY: Well, we're going to move to Canada as soon as we get married.

BRUCE: Oh, I see. What does your fiance do for a living?
MISS BRADLEY: He's a salesman. He often says that he'd earn far more if he were back in Canada. That's why he wants to go back.
BRUCE: But salesmen are quite well paid here in the States. How much does he make now, if I may ask?
MISS BRADLEY: About $125 a week.
BRUCE: That's not very much if he's a good salesman. You ought to tell him he'd earn a lot more if he came to work for us.
MISS BRADLEY: Well . . . uh . . . you see . . .
BRUCE: I mean, I'm sure that if I were a young salesman and if my salary were that low, I'd want to go someplace else too. Where does he work, by the way?
MISS BRADLEY: Uh . . . as a matter of fact, he works here in your factory, Mr. Foster. He's in your sales department.

Questions
1. Ask and answer these questions:
   a. Why / her job?
   b. stop working altogether?
   c. fiance come from?
   d. earn?
   e. Why / back to Canada?
2. What does Bruce say Miss Bradley ought to tell her fiance?
3. Where does he work?

Practice and Recall
Without looking at the text, see if you can remember how these phrases were used. Then try to make other sentences of your own with the same words.

a. I'm afraid it means
b. quit my job
c. It isn't that I . . .
d. for a living
e. by the way
f. as a matter of fact

e / Summary

Focal Points in this Unit

1. a. In this unit we have practiced another kind of Conditional sentence with the word *if* (If . . . did . . ., . . . would do). This is sometimes called the unreal Conditional, because, in a sentence like
    The job would be easy if that saw weren't broken,
    the fact is that the saw *is* broken and the job *isn't* easy.
    b. The verb in the *if* half of the sentence is in the Simple Past:
    If they *knew*, . . . / If he *had* a gun, . . . /
    If he *bought* a new suit, . . .
    c. The form of the verb in the other half of the sentence is *would* (*do*):
    . . . they *would start* screaming. / . . . it *would go* faster.

2. Remember that we only use a comma in the sentence if it begins with *if:*
    If they painted the house, it would look a lot better.

3. Remember the form of the verb *be* in this kind of sentence:
    If *I were* you, I would stay at home.
    We use *were* with all persons: If *I were* rich, . . . / If *he were* in your position, . . . / If *they were* here, . . ., etc.
    NOTE: In everyday conversation, you will often hear people say: "If he / she *was* . . .," instead of "If he / she *were* . . ."

f / Exercises for Homework

1. Do all the exercises on pages 129, 130 and 132.

2. Supply the correct form of the verb in parentheses in these sentences:
    a. If you (work) harder, you would earn more money.
    b. She (get) a much better job if she learned to type.
    c. If I (drink) coffee at night, I would stay awake all night.
    d. That house (probably look) very nice if they painted it.
    e. I'd drink a cup of coffee if you (make) some.

3. Give advice to the following people. Use "If I were you, I'd . . .":
    Example:
    A student who doesn't work very hard.
    Advice: **If I were you, I'd work a little harder.**
    a. A woman who always goes to bed very late.
    b. A friend who spends a lot of money on expensive clothes.
    c. A man who is very thin and unhealthy.
    d. A friend with a car that often breaks down.
    e. A man who is very unhappy with his job.
    f. Someone with a very bad toothache.
    g. A person who is trying to open a can with a screwdriver.
    h. A friend who has just bought a new car, and the car has just broken down.
    i. A man who wants a job in Venezuela, but can't speak Spanish.

4. **Guided Composition**
    A friend of yours has written to you recently to ask your advice about a problem. The problem is that the friend wants to brush up on his (or her) English, but doesn't know whether to go to a school in the U.S. for an intensive course or to go to evening classes in his (or her) country. Write a letter advising the friend what you would do.

5. **Transfer Exercise**
    Write down a number of things you would do right away if you won a lot of money.

1

a. Why / house look better?
b. Why / roof?
c. Why / gate?
d. Why / yard?
e. Who?
f. When?

2

a. When / these 3 cowboys?
b. know who?
c. How / Tom? How / Dick? How / Harry?

3

a. Who / Joe's favorite record?
b. When?
c. Susan / record?
d. What / Joe / say?

4

a. What / Joe / policeman?
b. What / happen? (bumper / headlight)
c. policeman's question?
d. Joe's answer?

5

a. When / storm?
b. How much damage? (trees / telephone wires / windows / a roof / a car)
c. When / all this?

6

a. When / Bruce's office?
b. money?
c. damage?

1

This is the same house we saw in Unit 22. It has been painted. The roof has been fixed. So has the gate. The yard looks better because the grass has been cut and some trees and bushes have been planted. We do not know who did all these things or even when they were done. All we can say is that they have been done.

1. What has happened to the house?
2. Ask and answer the same question for:
   a. the roof   b. the gate
3. Why does the yard look better?
4. There are two things we do not know; what are they?

2

These three cowboys were all killed a long time ago in Cactus City. These are their tombstones. We know how they died but not who killed them. All we can say is that Tom was hanged, Dick was shot and Harry was stabbed, all in 1877.

1. Correct the statements:
   a. We see the houses of three cowboys.
   b. They were killed a short time ago.
2. What do we know? What do we not know?
3. Ask and answer questions beginning "How was . . . killed?" and "When was . . . killed?"

3

Joe's favorite record has been broken. "It's been broken," he said a moment ago.

   "Well, don't look at me. I didn't break it," Susan said.

   "I didn't say you did. All I said was, 'It's been broken,' " Joe is saying now.

1. What has happened to Joe's record?
2. What are Joe's exact words when he notices this?
3. What is Susan's answer?
4. What is Joe saying now?
5. Why do you think he does not say "It was broken"?

4

Joe's car has been damaged. He is telling a policeman about it.

   "Look! The bumper's been bent and a headlight's been smashed!"

   "Do you know when this was done?"

   "No. All I know is the car was all right when I parked it here three hours ago!"

1. Ask and answer three questions beginning "Does he know when . . .?"
   a. the headlight   c. the bumper
   b. the car
2. What exactly is he saying about these three things?
3. What is the policeman's question?
4. What is the only thing Joe knows?

5

There was a terrible storm during the night. A lot of damage was done. Trees and telephone wires were blown down, windows were smashed and a roof was blown off. A car was even overturned. All this happened last night.

1. Ask and answer questions beginning "What happened to that / those . . . last night?"
2. Ask a question beginning "How much damage . . .?"
3. Suppose you have *just* seen all these things for the first time and perhaps do not know when they happened; what would you say?

6

Bruce's office was broken into this morning. Two secretaries are talking.

   "Have you heard? Mr. Foster's office has been broken into!"

   "I know. It was broken into this morning."

   "Was any money stolen?"

   "I think so. I know some damage was done."

1. How does the first secretary begin the conversation?
2. What does the other one say?
3. What exactly is the question with the words "any money"?

23b FORMATION AND MANIPULATION

1 Pronunciation

Be very careful with the pronunciation of the reduced form of *has* in contractions: *'s*

a. After words like *cat, cap, book, wife, path* (where the last sounds are unvoiced) *'s* is pronounced / s /.
   Example: The cat's (/ k æ ts /) been found.

b. After words like *head, thing, wave, tree, boy* (where the last sounds are voiced, vowels or diphthongs) *'s* is pronounced / z /.
   Example: The boy's (/ bɔyz /) been seen.

c. After words like *house, gaze, fish, church, judge,* the reduced form of *has* is pronounced / əz / or / ɨ z /.
   Example: The house has (/ hawsəz / or / haws ɨ z /) been painted.

2

A	B	C
The gate	has ('s) been	fixed.

a. Look at the situations on page 135 and find words to replace those in boxes A and C. (Of course, you'll have to change box B sometimes.)
b. Now say or write at least ten sentences.
c. Now, try to think of five new things to replace those in boxes A and C.
d. Look at this simple dialog: A: What's happened?
                                     B: The window's been broken.
e. Using the words you have found in exercises **a** and **c**, make these short dialogs with the person sitting next to you.
   Example: A: **What's happened?**
             B: **My car's been stolen.**

3

A	B	C
Some damage	was	done.

a. Make at least five sentences of your own by putting new words in boxes A and C. (Change *was* to *were* when necessary.)
b. Now make those sentences into questions beginning *When . . .?*
c. How many questions can you ask with *When . . .?* about the pictures on page 134?

4

It hasn't	been done	yet.

Make sentences using these words:

| my watch / repair | window / fix | radio / turn on |
| the house / sell | flowers / plant | car / wash |

The Man Who Escaped
EPISODE 23

SUMMARY: Kincaid told Fletcher that Hooper sold government secrets to other countries. Kincaid also told Fletcher that Hooper had planned what had happened to Fletcher in Philadelphia. He thought Fletcher would be killed in the crash and that the FBI would think he was a spy when they found the documents in his car.

Kincaid told Fletcher that Hooper owned a warehouse on the South Side of Chicago. It was also where the secret documents were kept before they were microfilmed and sent
5 abroad.

They got into Kincaid's car and drove there. Fletcher sat in front with Kincaid. Marilyn sat in the back. It was almost evening when they got to the warehouse. It was at the end of the
10 street and was surrounded by factories and other warehouses. People were beginning to go home. Fletcher sat and watched the lights go off. Fletcher turned to Kincaid again.

"Now tell me exactly where the documents
15 are kept," he said.

"They're kept in Hooper's office, in an ordinary file in his desk," he answered.

"And the microfilms?" Fletcher demanded.

"They're kept there too."
20 "Do you know if any documents have been sent anywhere recently?"

"Some were sent last week. I know. I sent them myself," Kincaid said.

"And will there be any there now, waiting to
25 be sent?"

Kincaid hesitated.

"I don't know. There might be. Hooper told me he was going to give me some tonight," he said.
30 Fletcher gave Marilyn the gun. She was still sitting behind Kincaid. "Keep him here until I get back," he said.

"But what are you going to do?" she asked.

"I'm going to break into the warehouse if I
35 can. Maybe I can find proof that Hooper sells these things. If I do, I'll phone the police."

"But what if you don't? What if somebody sees you? What if you're caught before you can find anything at all?" Marilyn asked. But
40 Fletcher had already started walking towards the warehouse. In the dark winter evening, it looked very much like a prison.

At the back of the warehouse, Fletcher found a drainpipe that led up to the roof. Once,
45 someone had told him that Army training was useful in many ways. Fletcher knew now that this was true. He was able to climb the drainpipe without difficulty. There was a skylight on the roof. It was closed but not locked. Fletcher
50 opened it carefully and peered down into the dark warehouse. There was a stack of large shipping crates directly below him. He jumped down onto them. He felt the stack of crates move from one side to the other. He tried to
55 keep his balance. Suddenly the whole stack crashed to the floor. Fletcher managed to jump off just in time, but the noise of the crates echoed throughout the warehouse. Then there was silence.

23d FURTHER PRACTICE

1 / For Comprehension

A. There has been another railroad accident in Nebraska. The accident occurred last night in freezing rain outside Omaha. Four people were killed and at least ten people were injured. The tracks have not yet been cleared and a number of trains have been delayed.

Questions
1. Where did the railroad accident occur?
2. Were there any casualties in the accident? (killed / injured)
3. Have the tracks been cleared yet?
4. Are the trains still running normally? (trains / delayed)

B. Heavy snow has fallen in northern Minnesota. Many roads have been blocked and traffic has been brought to a standstill. One town, Lancaster, has been completely cut off. Supplies will be dropped into the area by air this afternoon.

Questions
1. Where has heavy snow fallen?
2. What are conditions like? (many roads / traffic)
3. What has happened to Lancaster?

C. The office of Mr. J. P. Moore, the prominent industrialist, was broken into over the weekend. A small amount of money was taken and the office itself was left in what the office manager described as "a terrible mess." The burglary was discovered by employees early this morning. Mr. Moore is away on vacation in South America and has not yet been located.

Questions
1. What happened to Mr. Moore's office over the weekend?
2. Was any money taken?
3. How was the office left?
4. Who was the burglary discovered by?
5. When was the burglary discovered?

2 / Conversation

Joe Burns is a famous race car driver. He is being interviewed on a sports program.

REPORTER: You lead a very dangerous life, don't you, Joe? I mean, you've almost been killed several times, haven't you?

JOE: Yes. I suppose that's right.

REPORTER: When was your worst accident?

JOE: I'd say last year. It was during the Riviera Grand Prix. I smashed into a wall. The car was completely ruined and my left leg was broken. Luckily, nobody was killed.

REPORTER: Is that the only time you've been . . . uh . . . close to death?

JOE: No. Once, during the Mexican Grand Prix, two cars in front of me had a bad accident. One of them ran into the other. I swerved to avoid them and hit a fence. My car was badly damaged but luckily, I wasn't even hurt.

REPORTER: You must enjoy danger. I mean, you wouldn't be a race driver if you didn't, would you?

JOE: I don't know about that. I had a bad scare quite recently. I thought I was going to be killed at any moment.

REPORTER: Really? When was that? During your last race?

JOE: No. It was on my way to this television studio. I had to drive through New York during rush hour.

Questions
1. What has almost happened to Joe several times?
2. When was his worst accident? Describe it. (wall / car / leg)
3. What happened during the Mexican Grand Prix? (two cars / swerved / his car)
4. What did Joe think was going to happen to him very recently?
5. When did this last experience take place?

e / Summary

Focal Points in this Unit

1. Remember that we form the Passive in English with *be + past participle.* In this unit we have practiced two constructions: *has / have been done* and *was / were done.*

2. Remember that we use these two Passive constructions in the same way as we use the Active forms:
   a. *has / have been done + just, yet, ever, since, for* or no time.
      The house *has been painted* (since we last saw it).
   b. *was / were done + last night, yesterday, 3 weeks ago,* etc.
      Mr. Foster's office *was broken into* this morning.

3. We usually use the Passive when we don't know or don't want to say who has done, or who did something. If we use the Passive and still mention the person, however, we use the preposition *by*, as in the third news item on page 138: "The burglary *was discovered by* employees early this morning." In this sentence, the burglary is the most important piece of information.

f / Exercises for Homework

1. Do all the exercises on pages 135, 136 and 138.

2. Supply the correct form of the verb in parentheses (*has / have been done* or *was / were done*) in these sentences:
   a. The President (be shot) late last night.
   b. There isn't any food left. All of it (be eaten)!
   c. I can't find my car anywhere. I think it (be stolen)!
   d. Our house (be broken into) last week.
   e. Those paintings (be sold) last month for $1,000 each.
   f. His car (be damaged) in an accident last month.
   g. Have you heard? The old post office (be painted).
   h. That's a good book. It (be written) by James Michener.
   i. Because of bad weather yesterday, the traffic on Highway 10 (be brought) to a complete standstill.
   j. I (be frightened) to death when I drove through New York last month.

3. **Guided Composition**
   Read the first news item on page 138 again. Use that as a model and write about a bad car crash. Use these cues:
      car crash / Boston // yesterday afternoon / snowstorm / in the downtown area // one elderly lady / 4 other people / 2 cars / completely wrecked // not cleared / traffic / held up //

   Now read the second news item on page 138, and write a similar article beginning:
      Heavy rain has fallen . . .

4. **Transfer Exercise**
   Write 6 sentences about the news today, using the Passive.
   Examples:
   The President of . . . arrived in . . . today, and was met by the Secretary of State.

   . . . was beaten by . . . in the World Series baseball game in . . . today.

1

a. Where / Jane and Jim?
b. What / she / know?
c. Jane's question?
d. How / Jim / know / good restaurant?

2

a. How long / restaurant?
b. Why / Jane / angry?
c. What / Jim / the place?

3

a. What / always carry?
b. Where / Jim and Jane?
c. Where / money?
d. What / waiter?
e. Where / the manager?
f. Why / unfortunate?

4

a. What / Jim / minute ago?
b. personal checks?
c. What / explain?
d. Jim's words?
e. waiter's words?

5

a. Where / Joe?
b. What / Susan?
c. Susan's question: flowers?
d. Joe's answer? (worry / forget)

6

a. Why / Susan / upset?
b. What / tell Joe?

Told someone
Said

it was / did
she could / would do
they had been / had done

24a

1

Jane and Jim, her boyfriend, are outside a restaurant. Jane wants to know something before they go in.

"Are you sure it's a good restaurant?"

"Oh, yes!" Jim is saying, "I've been here before. It's very good. I know the owner and I always get good service."

1. Where are Jane and Jim?
2. Correct the statements:
   a. Jim says it is a bad place.
   b. He says he has never been here before.
   c. He says he does not know anyone.
   d. He says he never gets good service.

2

Jim and Jane have been in the restaurant for an hour and they still have not been waited on. Jane is angry. "You said this was a good place!" she is saying. "You said you had been here before! You said you knew the owner and always got good service!"

1. Where are Jane and Jim?
2. Ask "How long . . .?" and answer.
3. Why is Jane angry?
4. What did Jim say before they came in?
   a. good place   c. the owner
   b. before   d. good service

3

It is lucky that Jim always carries his checkbook with him. This is his conversation with a waiter in the restaurant where he and Jane have just had dinner:

"I'm sorry. I've left my money at home. But I have my checkbook with me."

"That's all right. You can write a check and give it to the cashier."

Unfortunately, the manager is standing at the cash register now, and he refuses to accept personal checks.

1. Why is it lucky that Jim carries his checkbook?
2. What are his exact words to the waiter?
3. What are the waiter's exact words?
4. What is going to happen at the cash register?
5. Ask if the waiter knows (and answer).

4

Jim handed his check to the manager a minute ago, and the manager shook his head and said he did not accept personal checks. Jim is explaining why he wrote a check.

"I told the waiter I'd left my money at home. He told me it didn't matter and that I could pay by check."

1. What did the manager say about personal checks?
2. What is Jim doing?
3. What did he tell the waiter?
4. What did the waiter tell him?

5

Joe is going downtown and Susan wants him to do something for her there.

"It's my mother's birthday tomorrow. Will you get her some flowers downtown? She loves roses."

Joe is saying, "Don't worry. I'll get her some! I won't forget!"

1. What does Susan want Joe to do?
2. Ask why (and answer).
3. Ask and answer these questions:
   a. When / birthday
   b. What kind of flowers
4. What is Joe saying?

6

Joe has come back from downtown but he has forgotten to get the roses. Susan is very upset.

"I told you it was my mother's birthday tomorrow and that she loved roses. You said you would get her some! You said you wouldn't forget!"

1. Ask why Susan is upset (and answer).
2. What did she tell him?
3. What did he say?
4. Correct the statements:
   a. He said he'd get them tomorrow.
   b. She said her mother's birthday was the next week.

141

24b FORMATION AND MANIPULATION

---

1 Notice the change:
IS / ARE / DOES

> Jim says, "This *is* a good restaurant."   Jim said it *was* a good restaurant.
> Jim says, "I *know* the owner."   He said he *knew* the owner.

Now make the same change yourself for these sentences that Jim says. Change them to *Jim said . . .*
a. "The food is good."
b. "The waiter speaks five languages."
c. "My boss often goes there."
d. "A lot of famous people eat there."
e. "The vegetables aren't fresh."
f. "The meat tastes strange."
g. "The soup has a funny taste."
h. "I don't like this place."

---

2 HAS / DONE / DID

> Jane says, "I'*ve left* my money at home."   Jane said she *had left* her money at home.
> or "I *left* my money at home."   Jane said she *left* her money at home.

Now change these statements to sentences beginning *Jane said . . .*
a. "I've lost my purse."
b. "I've broken my watch."
c. "I ate earlier."
d. "I knew Susan at school."
e. "The manager has already come."
f. "The bus has just left."
g. "The bus left 5 minutes early."
h. "My alarm clock didn't go off."

---

3 WILL DO / CAN DO

> Joe says, "I'*ll* get some downtown."   Joe said he *would* get some downtown.
> Joe says, "I *can* do it later."   He said he *could* do it later.

Now change these statements to sentences beginning *Joe said . . .*
a. "We can buy them later."
b. "I'll remember."
c. "I won't come home without them."
d. "Peter can get them."
e. "He'll be home soon."
f. "He won't mind."
g. "Susan will be very angry."
h. "I can't go home without them."

---

4 SAY / TELL
Notice that when we want to mention the person we said something to, we use the word *tell.*

> I said I was coming.
> I told you I was coming.

Now look at pictures 2, 4 and 6 on page 140. Ask questions like "What did . . . tell . . . earlier?"
Answer these questions with: "He / She told her / him that . . . "

The Man Who Escaped
EPISODE 24

SUMMARY: Kincaid told Fletcher that Hooper owned a warehouse on the South Side of Chicago. Fletcher, Marilyn and Kincaid went to the warehouse. Fletcher entered the warehouse through the skylight. When he jumped down onto a stack of crates, the crates fell over and made a lot of noise.

"That was lucky!" he told himself. "No one heard the noise."

"Kincaid told me the secrets were kept in the office, but where's the office?" he
5 wondered. Moving to the front of the warehouse, he came to several doors. One of them had the word "Manager" printed on it, and he knew that was Hooper's. It wasn't locked. He went to the desk on the other side
10 of the room. In the file he found several documents marked "Top Secret."

"Here's my proof!" he told himself excitedly. Suddenly he heard a sound behind him.

15 Before he could turn around, something struck him and he felt an explosion of pain in his head. Just before he lost consciousness, he realized that what had happened in Philadelphia was happening to him all over
20 again.

When he came to, he was lying on the floor in the middle of the warehouse. He had no idea how long he had been there. He heard loud voices. Raising his head slightly, he saw
25 Marilyn tied to a chair, and four men standing a few feet away. One of them was Kincaid, looking pale and frightened. He was listening to a short blond man. Fletcher knew it must be Hooper. Hooper was shouting.
30 "I told you you were a fool! You idiot! Do you believe me now?" he demanded. Kincaid tried to say something but he could not.

Hooper hit him in the face.

"I asked you a question!" he shouted.

"But . . . Hooper, pl . . . please listen to
35 me!" Kincaid stammered. "I told you some-one had phoned me and asked me to look at some pistols! I told you it was an old man and you said there was nothing to worry about!"

"No, I didn't. I asked you what you wanted
40 me to do about it, you idiot!" Hooper yelled.

Suddenly, one of the men interrupted.

"What are we going to do with the girl and Fletcher?" he asked.

45 "We're going to kill them! And we're going to do the job right this time!" Hooper answered.

All of a sudden, Hooper noticed that Fletch-er's eyes were open. Taking out his gun, he
50 pointed it down at Fletcher.

24d FURTHER PRACTICE

1 / For Comprehension

Read this newspaper article and answer the questions.

When Senator John Hawkins was asked about compulsory education again at a press conference yesterday, he said that there were still a large number of problems to be considered. One reporter asked what school boards could do about children who wanted to go out and earn money at the age of 16. Senator Hawkins said that he realized a lot of young people wanted to stand on their own two feet early in life, and he thought this was very admirable. But he added that he felt young people needed as much education as we could give them; so he said he would not be in favor of lowering the age limit for compulsory education.

Questions

1. Where was Senator Hawkins yesterday?
2. What was he asked about?
3. What did he say about "a large number of problems"?
4. Write down the exact words which one reporter used when he asked Senator Hawkins about compulsory education.
5. What did Senator Hawkins say a lot of young people wanted to do?
6. What did he think about this?
7. What did he say about young people and education?
8. What is the Senator's attitude toward lowering the age limit for compulsory education?

2 / Conversation

Most of Bruce's employees at the Foster Shoe Company are between 18 and 45. Most of them are serious workers too. A few are not. Bruce is talking with one of the few now. She has just told him that she can't come to work tomorrow because her grandmother is sick.

BRUCE: You've already missed far too many days this month, Miss Grey.

MISS GREY: Yes, I know I have. I'm very sorry. You see, I have these terrible headaches and . . .

BRUCE: Headaches? Last week you said you had trouble with your stomach!

MISS GREY: Uh . . . well . . . you see, I have headaches *and* trouble with my stomach. That's why I've been out so often.

BRUCE: And you often come to work late as well. Yesterday, for instance, you . . .

MISS GREY: Yes. I'm very sorry about that. You see, my alarm clock didn't go off and . . .

BRUCE: Your alarm clock? But you told me yesterday that the bus had broken down!

MISS GREY: Oh, did I? Well . . . uh . . . I suppose I just forgot to say that my alarm clock hadn't gone off either.

BRUCE: It's a very complicated story, if you'll forgive me saying so, Miss Grey. Now, tell me again why you want tomorrow off.

MISS GREY: Well . . . uh . . . you see . . . my grandfather's sick. He's in the hospital and . . . and he's going to have an operation. I want to visit him.

BRUCE: Oh, I see. So your grandfather's sick too.

MISS GREY: I don't understand.

BRUCE: Neither do I, Miss Grey. When we began this conversation, you said your *grandmother* was sick. And you didn't say she was going to have an operation! You said she'd already had one! And by the way, you also said she was in a nursing home, not in a hospital!

Questions

1. Miss Grey has missed work a lot. What reason did she give last week?
2. What reason did she give for being late yesterday?
3. What did she say about her grandmother earlier?

Practice

Go through the Conversation again. Find all the examples you can that begin with *you said* or *you told me*. Then say what the exact words were at the time Miss Grey first said these things.

24e/f

e / Summary

Focal Points in this Unit

1. Remember how we use the two verbs *say* and *tell:*
   a. *I said* is simply followed by the reported information.
   b. We add a person (*him / her / us / John*, etc.) after *I told.*

   Compare these two sentences:

   He *said* he would be late.
   He *told me* he would be late.

2. Remember that verbs in the past after *said* or *told him* go back one tense from what was said originally:

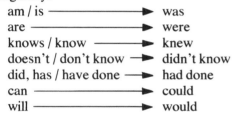

   am / is ⟶ was
   are ⟶ were
   knows / know ⟶ knew
   doesn't / don't know ⟶ didn't know
   did, has / have done ⟶ had done
   can ⟶ could
   will ⟶ would

   Example:
   Original statement: "I don't know."
   Reported statement: He said he didn't know.

f / Exercises for Homework

1. Do all the exercises on pages 141, 142 and 144.

2. Change these sentences into Reported Speech.
   Example:
   "I'm a singer," she said.
   You write: **She said she was a singer.**
   a. "I like tea," she said.
   b. "I hate it," he told me.
   c. "John never wears a dark suit," she said.
   d. "I think that is a very good idea," he said.
   e. "You can write a check," the waiter told him.
   f. "You are a fool," Hooper told Kincaid.
   g. "I'll buy a new suit if I get the job," the young man said.
   h. "My car has broken down," he told the mechanic.
   i. "I'm going to get more rest!" he told the doctor.
   j. "I've just been to the dentist," he told me when I saw him a minute ago. (Begin: When I saw him a minute ago, . . .)

3. Read this passage and write down exactly what they said:

   When I woke up, I asked my wife what the weather was like. She looked out the window and said it was raining pretty hard, but she thought it was going to clear up. Later, when we were having breakfast, I listened to the weather forecast. The forecaster said that weather conditions would probably be variable. He added that it was difficult to say when the weather would become more stable. My wife said that was fine because she had decided to stay home and do some baking.

4. **Guided Composition**
   Read the Conversation between Mr. Foster and Miss Grey on page 144 again. Think of an excuse for being late for school, college or work. Write down how you told a friend what happened when you used the excuse to your teacher or to your boss. Report what you said and what he or she said. Begin like this:

   I was late for school (or college or work) again last . . . When I went in, . . .

5. **Transfer Exercise**
   Report a number of things that different people have said to you in the past couple of days. For example, if a friend said to you yesterday, "I'm going to a party tonight," you write:

   My friend told me he was going to a party last night.

145

1

a. time now?
b. Joe / movie?
c. Why not?

2

a. When / Fred?
b. other soldier's question?
c. Fred's answer?

3

a. When / Peter / from Europe?
b. job yet?
c. What / Joe / say?
d. What / Peter / think?

4

a. Why / Jones / dead?
b. Jones's explanation?

5

a. When / woman / curb?
b. What / if / driver?
c. What / second and third cars?
d. What / if / woman / careful

1

It is 9 o'clock. Susan has just asked, "Aren't you going to watch the movie?" Unfortunately, Joe has a lot of work to do. "I would if I had the time," he answers.

It is 11 o'clock. The movie is over. Joe did not watch it. He would have watched it if he had had the time.
1. What is Susan's question at 9:00?
2. What is Joe's answer?
3. What can we say about Joe at 11:00?

2

Fred joined the army six months ago. At that time he did not know how hard life was going to be for him. Another soldier has just asked him a question.

"Would you have joined if you had known?"

"No, I wouldn't," Fred answers.
1. What happened 6 months ago?
2. What was it that Fred did not know then?
3. What is the other soldier's question and what is Fred's answer?
4. Correct the statements:
   a. He knew how hard life was going to be.
   b. He would still have joined if he had known.

3

Peter came back from Europe six months ago. He has not found a job yet. His brother Joe often tells him,

"You would have found a job a long time ago if you had looked harder!"

Peter often says, "Perhaps it would have been better if I'd stayed in Europe!"
1. Ask and answer the questions:
   a. When / from Europe?
   b. a job yet?
2. What does Joe often tell Peter?
3. What does Peter often say?

4

We saw this scene earlier. When Sheriff Jones came into the bar, a stranger made a sudden move. Jones shot him dead. The man only wanted to look at his watch. Jones is explaining,

"I'd never have shot him if he hadn't made a sudden move. If he hadn't been a stranger, I wouldn't have been so suspicious."
1. Why was Jones so suspicious?
2. Ask and answer a question with *if*. (suspicious / a stranger)
3. What did the stranger do when Jones came in?
4. Ask another question with *if* and answer. (shot him / sudden move)

5

A few seconds ago, that woman suddenly stepped off the curb. The first car would have hit her if the driver had not stopped just in time. Unfortunately, the second car crashed into him and the third car swerved and hit the curb. The first driver has lost his temper, the second driver has damaged both cars and the third has knocked down a telephone pole. None of this would have happened if the woman had been more careful. Unfortunately, the damage has been done now.
1. What happened a few seconds ago?
2. Make as many sentences as you can beginning "If the woman had been more careful . . ."
3. Ask as many questions as you can like this:
   "Would the first driver have stopped so suddenly if the woman hadn't stepped out in front of his car?"

25b FORMATION AND MANIPULATION

1 Pronunciation
   a. Notice the pronunciation of *have* in the last sentence of situation 1, page 147:
   He would have / əv / (sometimes written *would've*) watched it if . . .
   b. Notice the pronunciation of *had* in the last line of situation 1, page 147, where the word *had* occurs twice. The first *had* may be pronounced in its contracted form (*'d*). but the second *had* must be stressed (in its full form):
   . . . if he had had ('d h æ d) the time.

2

A	B	C	D	E
He would have	watched it	if	he'd	had the time.

   a. Think of words to replace those in boxes B and E. You'll find some in the situations on page 147 and also in the other conditional situations on page 129.
   b. Look at this simple exchange:
   "Did he watch it?"
   "No, he didn't, but he would have watched it if he'd had the time."
   c. Now, using the words you have found in exercise **a**, think up at least ten examples of the dialog in exercise **b**. You should do this orally with the person sitting next to you and also write down a few examples (two or three).

3

A	B	C	D
Would you have	joined	if you had	known?

   a. By using pages 147 and 129 again, find words to replace those in boxes B and D. (You can, of course, change *you* in A and C.)
   b. With the words you have found in exercise **a**, write or ask at least ten questions like the example above.
   c. Now practice asking the same ten questions starting with *if.*
   Example: **If you had known, would you have joined?**

4

A	B	C	D
If he hadn't	been a stranger,	I wouldn't have	been so suspicious.

   a. Think of other words to go in boxes B and D.
   b. Change *he* and *I* in boxes A and D as necessary.
   c. First write or say at least ten sentences using the words you have found in exercises **a** and **b**.
   d. Now, write the same sentences, or some new ones, starting with boxes C and D.
   Example: **I wouldn't have been so suspicious if he hadn't been a stranger.**

The Man Who Escaped

EPISODE 25

SUMMARY: *Inside the warehouse, Fletcher found Hooper's office. Looking in Hooper's desk, he found the secret documents he was looking for. Just at that moment, however, someone hit him on the head and knocked him out. When he woke up, he saw Marilyn tied to a chair and he heard Hooper shouting at Kincaid. As soon as Hooper noticed that Fletcher's eyes were open, he pointed a gun at him.*

"Get him on that chair!" Hooper ordered. Two men immediately grabbed Fletcher. They put him in a chair and they tied his hands behind his back.

5 "You'd never have bothered us again if I'd used *this* four years ago," he said. He came closer to Fletcher and aimed the gun at his head.

"We would never have become suspicious if 10 you hadn't used Kincaid's car," he said. "When we saw it parked down the street, we decided to wait and see what would happen. Then after we got you, we went out and got your girlfriend," he continued.

15 "If you thought you could ruin my operation after all these years, you were wrong!"

Fletcher knew he would never have made such a stupid mistake if he had not been so tired. He had not gotten much sleep for the 20 past few days. He looked at Marilyn. "I'd never have gotten you into all this if I hadn't asked you for help," he said to her. They were trapped. It seemed there was nothing he could do and there was nobody who could help them.

25 Suddenly there was a terrific crash as three policemen broke down the side door of the warehouse. Hooper turned around, ready to shoot. "No, Hooper. Look over here!" a voice yelled from the other end of the warehouse. 30 Suddenly, everybody froze. Nobody made a move. Then Rossi walked toward them, followed by Wilcox.

"Take his gun, Wilcox," Rossi said calmly.

"I was only protecting my property," 35 Hooper answered. "This man broke into my warehouse. That woman helped him. Arrest them!" Rossi listened and smiled.

"We've been here for nearly half an hour," he said. "We've heard everything—enough to 40 put you and Kincaid in prison for a long, long time."

The policemen suddenly moved forward and seized Hooper, Kincaid and the three other men. One of them untied Marilyn and Fletcher.

45 "It's a lucky thing for you, Fletcher, that we got here when we did!" Rossi said.

"How did you find us?" Fletcher asked.

"You mean you didn't know I was coming?" Rossi joked.

50 Fletcher went back to Hooper's office and got the documents.

"Here's something I want you to see," he said, handing them to Rossi.

"What we know now proves you are 55 innocent," Rossi said. "I'm going to have to take you back to Leavenworth, but a special meeting of the Board of Pardons will be arranged."

Fletcher was silent. "What about Marilyn? I 60 got her into all of this . . . ."

"Everything's going to be all right," Rossi answered. "Nobody can give you back the four years you spent in prison, but at least it's over now."

65 Fletcher breathed a deep sigh of relief. "It's true . . . it's really true . . . !" he told himself. "I'm free again!"

THE END

1 / Invention Exercise

Make sentences with ". . . would / wouldn't have done . . . if . . . had / hadn't done."

CUE: that movie / time

RESPONSE: **I would have seen that movie if I had had the time.**

or: **We would have gone to see that movie if we had found the time.**

CUE: accident / asleep

RESPONSE: **He wouldn't have had an accident if he hadn't fallen asleep.**

or: **I would have had an accident if I had fallen asleep.**

Cues:

a. that job / a haircut
b. so suspicious / a stranger
c. some flowers / enough money
d. football / leg
e. the book / the movie
f. married / the right man
g. train / bus / so slow
h. money / savings account
i. university / army
j. job / carefully

2 / Conversation

Peter, Joe and Susan have all gone to a very expensive restaurant. They've just finished eating.

SUSAN: I have to admit your roast beef looked even better than my steak. I think I would have ordered that if I'd known.

JOE: Do you mean you didn't like the steak?

SUSAN: Oh, no. Just the opposite. I enjoyed my meal very much.

PETER: Well, I'm glad you both enjoyed it because I'm going to pay for this. Waiter!

JOE: Don't be silly, Peter! We can't let you do that.

SUSAN: No, we can't. I mean, we'd never have come to such an expensive place if you'd told us that earlier.

PETER: No, let me pay. I insist.

WAITER: Yes, sir. Would you like anything else?

PETER: No, just the check, please.

WAITER: Uh . . . separate checks or all together?

PETER: All together, of course.

WAITER: Fine. I'll be right back.

PETER: What a strange question. It's my long hair; otherwise, he'd never have asked me that.

JOE: What do you mean?

PETER: Oh, it's just that all these snobbish waiters think people like me never have any money.

SUSAN: He's coming back now.

PETER: Oh, no!

JOE: What's wrong?

PETER: I haven't got any money! I must have left it at home. I . . . uh . . . I'd never have offered to pay if I'd known. Do you think you could lend me some money, Joe?

Questions

1. What would Susan have done if she had known about the roast beef?
2. What does Susan say when Peter tells them he is going to pay?
3. What does the waiter ask when Peter asks for the check?
4. What is Peter's comment?
5. What does Peter notice just before the waiter comes back?
6. What does he ask Joe to do?

e / Summary

Focal Points in this Unit

1. In this unit, we have practiced another kind of Conditional sentence with the word *if* (*If . . . had done, . . . would have done*). This is sometimes called the Past Conditional because when we use it, we are always talking about the past. Like the other Conditional sentences we practiced in Unit 22, however, this is also *unreal*. In a sentence like *I'd never have shot him if he hadn't made a sudden move*, the fact is that the stranger really made a sudden move, and the sheriff shot him!

2. Remember that the verb in the *if* half of the sentence is in the Past Perfect tense:
   If I *had stayed* at home, . . .

3. Remember that the verb in the other half of the sentence is *would have done*:
   If I had stayed at home, I *would have watched* that program on television.

4. Remember that the reduced form of both *would* and *had* is *'d*. Look at this sentence:
   I'd (I would) never have done that if *I'd* (I had) known.

f / Exercises for Homework

1. Do all the exercises on pages 147, 148 and 150.

2. Complete these sentences:
   a. If I had known, . . .
   b. We wouldn't have gone there . . .
   c. If we hadn't been in such a hurry, . . .
   d. I wouldn't have asked them . . .
   e. If the prices hadn't gone up so much, . . .

3. Make comments to the following people. Use "I wouldn't have . . . if I had been you."
   Example:
   A friend who failed an exam because he wasted time.

Comment: **I wouldn't have wasted so much time if I had been you.**
   a. A person who paid $1,500 for a car that was only really worth $500.
   b. A friend who went on a 3-week vacation, but who spent all his (or her) money in the first week.
   c. A man who is tired this morning because he stayed up too late last night.
   d. A friend who went for an interview for an office job and wore an old sweater and jeans and not a suit.
   e. A friend who was arrested by the police because he was involved in a violent political demonstration.

4. Look at these two sentences:
   You'd never have bothered us again if I'd used this four years ago.
   We would never have become suspicious if you hadn't used Kincaid's car.
   Now write about other incidents from *The Man Who Escaped* and say what the consequences would or wouldn't have been if . . . (something else had or hadn't happened). Here are some reminders:
   a. Mrs. Bentley's old truck
   b. Fletcher getting off the freight train before Jefferson City
   c. Fletcher's plan to make Kincaid come to the hotel
   d. Rossi arriving at Hooper's warehouse in Chicago

5. **Transfer Exercise**
   Do you remember sentences like *I had no idea it was going to be so crowded?*
   We practiced a lot of sentences like this in Unit 20. Write some true sentences using "would / wouldn't have done . . . if . . . had done + was / were going to."
   Example:
   I wouldn't have gone to the football game if I had known it was going to be so boring.

Irregular Verbs

Infinitive	Past Tense	Past Participle	Infinitive	Past Tense	Past Participle
be	was / were	been	let	let	let
beat	beat	beaten	lie	lay	lain
become	became	become	light	lit (lighted)	lit (lighted)
begin	began	begun	lose	lost	lost
bend	bent	bent	make	made	made
bet	bet	bet	mean	meant	meant
bite	bit	bitten	meet	met	met
blow	blew	blown	put	put	put
break	broke	broken	quit	quit	quit
bring	brought	brought	read	read	read
build	built	built	ride	rode	ridden
buy	bought	bought	ring	rang	rung
catch	caught	caught	rise	rose	risen
choose	chose	chosen	run	ran	run
come	came	come	say	said	said
cost	cost	cost	see	saw	seen
cut	cut	cut	sell	sold	sold
dig	dug	dug	send	sent	sent
do	did	done	set	set	set
draw	drew	drawn	shake	shook	shaken
drink	drank	drunk	shine	shone (shined)	shone (shined)
drive	drove	driven	shoot	shot	shot
eat	ate	eaten	shut	shut	shut
fall	fell	fallen	sing	sang	sung
feed	fed	fed	sink	sank	sunk
feel	felt	felt	sit	sat	sat
fight	fought	fought	sleep	slept	slept
find	found	found	slide	slid	slid
fit	fit (fitted)	fit (fitted)	speak	spoke	spoken
fly	flew	flown	spend	spent	spent
forget	forgot	forgotten	stand	stood	stood
freeze	froze	frozen	steal	stole	stolen
get	got	got (gotten)	stick	stuck	stuck
give	gave	given	strike	struck	struck
go	went	gone	swear	swore	sworn
hang	hung	hung	sweep	swept	swept
have	had	had	swim	swam	swum
hear	heard	heard	take	took	taken
hide	hid	hidden	teach	taught	taught
hit	hit	hit	tear	tore	torn
hold	held	held	tell	told	told
hurt	hurt	hurt	think	thought	thought
keep	kept	kept	throw	threw	thrown
know	knew	known	understand	understood	understood
lay	laid	laid	wake	woke	woke / woken
lead	led	led	wear	wore	worn
leave	left	left	win	won	won
lend	lent	lent	write	wrote	written